Praise for the

There is no doubt that this w ... crisis. The ecological and sociological reality we're living in and must face up to is quite frankly terrifying. Yet there is hope. The authors of the *Earth Spirit* series from Moon Books show us that there are solutions to be found in ecological and eco-spiritual practices. I recommend this series to anyone who is concerned about our current situation and wants to find some hope in solutions they can practice for themselves.

Sarah Kerr, Pagan Federation President

This bold and rich *Earth Spirit* series provides vital information, perspectives, poetry and wisdom to guide and support through the complex environmental, climate and biodiversity challenges and crisis facing us all. Nothing is avoided within the wide range of author views, expertise and recommendations on eco-spirituality. I am deeply inspired by the common call, across the books, to radically change our relationship with the planet to a more respectful, mutual, spiritual and sustainable way of living; both individually and collectively. Each book offers its own particular flavour and practical offering of solutions and ways forward in these unprecedented times. Collectively the series provides an innovative, inspiring and compelling compendium of how to live, hope and act from both ancient and modern wisdoms. Whatever your views, concerns and aspirations for your life, and for the planet, you will find something of value. My life and understanding is deeply enhanced through the privilege of reading this series.

Dr Lynne Sedgmore CBE, Founder of Goddess Luminary Leadership Wheel, Executive Coach, Priestess and ex Chief Executive

In a world that is faced with such immense environmental issues, we can often feel paralysed and impotent. The *Earth Spirit* series is a welcome and inspiring antidote to fear and apathy. These books gift us with positive and inspiring visions that serve to empower and strengthen our own resolve to contribute to the healing of our planet, our communities and ourselves.
Eimear Burke, Chosen Chief of The Order of Bards, Ovates and Druids

Thanks to Moon Books and an amazing group of authors for stepping up in support of our need to address, with grace and aliveness, the ecological crises facing humanity. We must take concerted, focused, positive action on every front NOW, and this is best and most powerfully done when we base our offerings in a deep sense of spirit. White Buffalo Woman came to us 20 generations ago, reminding us of the importance of a holy perception of the world – based in Oneness, unity, honor and respect. Even as that is profound, it is also practical, giving us a baseline of power from which to give our gifts of stewardship and make our Earth walk a sacred one – for us and for All Our Relations. Walk in Beauty with these authors!
Brooke Medicine Eagle, Earthkeeper and author of *Buffalo Woman Comes Singing* and *The Last Ghost Dance*

Earth Spirit is an exciting and timely series. It has never been more important to engage with ideas that promote a positive move forward for our world. Our planet needs books like these – they offer us heartening signposts through the most challenging of times.
Philip Carr-Gomm, author of *Druid Mysteries, Druidcraft* and *Lessons in Magic*

Our relationship to the Mother Earth and remembering our roles as caretakers and guardians of this sacred planet is essential in weaving ourselves back into the tapestry of our own sacred nature. From the shamanic perspective, we are not separate from nature. The journey to finding solutions for the Earth will come through each person's reconnection to her heartbeat and life force.

Chandra Sun Eagle, author of *Looking Back on the Future*

This is important work as we humans face one of the greatest challenges in our collective history.

Ellen Evert Hopman, Archdruid of Tribe of the Oak and author of *A Legacy of Druids, A Druid's Herbal of Sacred Tree Medicine, The Sacred Herbs of Spring*, and other volumes

EARTH SPIRIT

Eco-Spirituality and Human–Animal Relationships

EARTH SPIRIT
Eco-Spirituality and Human–Animal Relationships

Mark Hawthorne

**MOON
BOOKS**

Winchester, UK
Washington, USA

JOHN HUNT PUBLISHING

First published by Moon Books, 2022
Moon Books is an imprint of John Hunt Publishing Ltd., No. 3 East Street, Alresford
Hampshire SO24 9EE, UK
office@jhpbooks.net
www.johnhuntpublishing.com
www.moon-books.net

For distributor details and how to order please visit the 'Ordering' section on our website.

Text copyright: Mark Hawthorne 2021

ISBN: 978 1 78535 248 5
978 1 78535 249 2 (ebook)
Library of Congress Control Number: 2021947906

A CIP catalogue record for this book is available from the British Library.

Design: Matthew Greenfield

UK: Printed and bound by CPI Group (UK) Ltd, Croydon, CR0 4YY
Printed in North America by CPI GPS partners

We operate a distinctive and ethical publishing philosophy in
all areas of our business, from our global network of authors to
production and worldwide distribution.

Contents

Introduction   1

Chapter 1 – Animals Used for Food   5
Chapter 2 – Animals in Captivity   13
Chapter 3 – Animals in Labs   25
Chapter 4 – Animals for Sport   40
Chapter 5 – Animals for Labor   48
Chapter 6 – Animals We Revere   61

About the Author   73

Introduction

The change was nothing less than extraordinary. In 2020 and 2021, the COVID-19 pandemic made its way around the world, leading to a drastic decline in human activity. Forced to shelter in place much of the time, people no longer filled shopping malls, restaurants, and pubs. If they could, employees worked from home; many businesses went dark. Especially significant were travel restrictions. The flow of transportation – airplanes, automobiles, trains, and boats – was reduced to a trickle.

This so-called anthropause had a remarkable impact on other species and the environment. In a world drastically slowed down, the near absence of human mobility allowed animals to relax and exhibit new behaviors. Wildlife began appearing in daylight, wandering deserted urban landscapes. Lions and leopards reclined within African safari resorts. Endangered sea turtles, who lay their eggs on beaches often crowded with tourists, experienced a boom in their numbers. Dugongs – a threatened marine mammal closely related to the manatee – returned to feed in Thai waters normally congested with speedboats. In Japan's Nara Park, home to more than 1,200 free-roaming sika deer used to subsisting on rice crackers from visitors, elder members of the herd guided their offspring to grassy meadows where they had grazed decades earlier; soon their normally watery droppings resembled firm black beans, indicating the deer were enjoying a healthier natural diet.

The lockdown and reduction in human activity had an equally dramatic effect on air and water quality. Within a month, China saw levels of nitrogen oxide (a greenhouse gas far more potent than carbon dioxide) drop 40 percent. Los Angeles soon became smog-free, albeit briefly. Residents in India's ancient city of Jalandhar could see the Himalayas, a hundred or so miles in the distance, for the first time in 30 years. The murky canals of Venice became clear enough for aquatic animals – including a nearly transparent jellyfish – to be spotted swimming in it. The Hudson River in New York was so clean that researchers could see the difference from space.

It was as if some divine being had pressed the Earth's reset button, giving us a glimpse of what the world could be like without human interference. Not a utopia, perhaps, but certainly more habitable and harmonious.

Yet as the lockdown benefitted Earth and her animals, it also harmed them. Emboldened by fewer armed patrols to observe their activities, for instance, poachers had an easier time killing rhinos and other species. Conservation programs struggled for funding. Loggers began plundering protected forests. And lazy humans found a new and abundant product they could litter the land with: protective face masks.

If anything, the anthropause was a lesson in what *could be*. Even the most optimistic among us probably realized that once the COVID-19 pandemic had passed, humans would return to business as usual. Cars and trucks would reemerge to jam highways. Noise pollution from boats would again stress marine life. A brown, stinging haze would reappear over cities. Animals would go back into hiding.

Some of us were perhaps moved by how the world had temporarily changed. Maybe we considered how life could be different. After all, there was much discussion, from scientists as well as pundits, about how the pandemic had been caused by humanity's exploitation of animals – and that more viruses like COVID-19 are likely if we don't alter our relationship with animals.

Clearly, the lives of humans and the lives of animals intersect in so many ways. Our connection with other species is probably best described as complicated. There are those animals we bond with and heap our affection on; we call them pets, companion animals, or even refer to them as our "kids." There are wild animals we admire from afar, in awe of their beauty and strength. And there are those animals we use for a wide variety of purposes: food, entertainment, research, and more. All major religions profess that there is a spiritual dimension to our relationship with the natural world – and protection of animals is a core principle – yet religions are notorious for exploiting animals as well, which is at best counterintuitive and at worst hypocritical.

As we view our relationship with animals (and, indeed, all of Nature) through the lens of eco-spirituality, we must ask ourselves what we can do to help heal the damage humanity has done to them. What responsibility do we have to not only reverse climate change, end deforestation, clean the ocean, and halt species extinction, but to ensure that the habits, practices, and choices that brought us to this crisis point are not repeated by future generations – and how can eco-spirituality help?

For the benefit of the uninitiated, eco-spirituality is simply another way of centering the sacred in Nature. This has been fundamental to the traditions of Indigenous people such as Native Americans. But as practiced by Europeans, it is a philosophy with roots that reach back to St. Francis of Assisi (c. 1181–1226), recognized for his love of animals; to the pantheism of Baruch Spinoza (1632–1677); and more recently to the works of naturalist Henry David Thoreau (1817–1862). Eco-spirituality seeks to reassess our relationship with the environment, where humans are not morally superior but rather equal to the life forms with whom we share this planet. The goal, then, is to truly live in harmony with Nature.

That is something we have struggled with for millennia. Animal bones found in Tanzania in 2012 suggest that early human ancestors were stalking, killing, and eating animals at least two million years ago. This hardly classifies as a "relationship," of course, and it would be a long time before animals and human beings formed a mutually beneficial connection, but we can infer from the earliest known cave paintings that our ancient ancestors had a preoccupation with our fellow beings.

In the following six chapters, we will explore humanity's multilayered relationship with animals. We will consider the ways we use animals, such as for entertainment and as a source of protein, and we will look at animals we admire, including wildlife, and those we form mutually beneficial bonds with: our animal companions.

Our kinship with animals has perhaps always been fragmented, but it's not too late to embrace a new paradigm. For us, for them, and for the planet.

Chapter 1

Animals Used for Food

But for the sake of some little mouthful of flesh we deprive a soul of the sun and light, and of that proportion of life and time it had been born into the world to enjoy. – Plutarch

Nowhere does the relationship between humans and non-human animals intersect as often (and some would argue as powerfully) as at the dinner table. Not everyone has a companion animal, not everyone has a daily encounter with wildlife, not everyone even hears a bird outside their window each morning – but nearly every human on Earth consumes meat, dairy, and/or eggs at least once a day. They do so principally without giving any thought to what life might have been like for the animal from which it came.

Each year, an estimated 70 billion land animals are slaughtered for food.[1] These are animals humans have essentially engineered – that is, they have been bred, raised, and modified specifically to serve as a source of protein. Most of them are chickens, and most of these chickens live in vast enterprises hidden from public view. It's just about the most abnormal existence you could imagine, where animals are confined in tight spaces and denied nearly every natural instinct and behavior.

According to legend, the modern era of animal agriculture began in 1923, when a small backyard farmer named Celia Steele placed her annual order of 50 chickens from a nearby hatchery to be delivered to her home in Delaware. Back then, chickens were primarily raised for their eggs, not their flesh, and they spent much of their time outdoors. But when Steele's order arrived by post, she had not 50 but 500 chickens.

Rather than return 450 chickens to the hatchery, Steele

decided to build a chicken house, raise the flock as so-called "broilers," and sell them to restaurants. The following year, she ordered 1,000 chickens, and as word spread of her success, other farmers got into the "broiler" business.[2]

Modern animal agriculture – with tens of thousands of animals being raised and confined in massive barns – resembles nothing so much as a factory, which is why animal advocates commonly refer to these enterprises as factory farms or animal factories. Farmers from a few generations ago would probably not recognize the scale of these operations as anything like what they were familiar with. In 1925, as Celia Steele was reinventing the industry, it took about 16 weeks to raise a broiler for market; by the 1990s, that timeline had been reduced to less than seven weeks. Meanwhile, the size of these birds going to slaughter had increased from 2.5 pounds in 1925 to nearly six and a half pounds today.[3] Chickens raised for meat are now so unnaturally heavy that they suffer from a variety of health problems. "Broilers are the only livestock that are in chronic pain for the last 20 percent of their lives," said John Webster, professor emeritus at the University of Bristol. "They don't move around, not because they are overstocked, but because it hurts their joints so much."[4]

Climate Change

The consequences of animal agriculture are not just detrimental to the animals but to the environment. There's a lot of information in the news and online about how much the production of meat, dairy, and eggs creates greenhouse gases and contributes to climate change, and much of that information is confusing at best and downright deceptive at worst. What is clear is that scientists tend to agree that avoiding animal consumption and moving toward a plant-based diet would have a profound impact on the health of our planet.

Let's take one measure as an example. According to a report by the Intergovernmental Panel on Climate Change – a body of the United Nations dedicated to providing objective, scientific information regarding human-induced climate change – a worldwide shift to plant-based diets would potentially reduce global emissions from our current level of 55.3 gigatonnes of carbon dioxide equivalent (abbreviated as $GtCO_2e$) per year to 8 $GtCO_2e$ per year.[5]

One of the reasons that animal agriculture has such a negative impact on the environment is that ruminant animals such as cows and sheep produce significant amounts of methane, a greenhouse gas, as they digest food – anywhere from 250 to 500 liters per animal per day[6] – and methane is 34 times more potent than carbon dioxide (CO_2).[7]

The full impact of industrialized agriculture on the planet is often hidden. When we think of meat production, for instance, we don't often consider the land that was deforested to make room for the animals to graze. Nor do we think of the land cleared so that animal feed such as soybeans could be planted and harvested. Did you know that trees and plants actually absorb CO_2 as food? It happens during photosynthesis: as the leaves pull in CO_2 and water, they use the power of the sun to convert them into nutrients – and in the process, they release oxygen. You can imagine the aftermath of clearing swathes of the Amazon rainforest, which acts as a massive carbon sink that also dampens the global temperature.

So, when you hear someone say they went vegan for the environment, this is what they are talking about! Yes, cell-based meat, also known as lab-grown meat, promises new approaches to animal protein and, consequently, to our kinship with animals. But why eat *any* animal products when there are so many delicious and nutritious plant-based foods available?

Youth Ag Programs

Arguably no relationship between humans and animals raised for food is more complicated than the bond often seen between children and the farmed animals they nurture for agricultural youth programs found in the National 4-H Council (part of the United States Department of Agriculture) and the National FFA Organization (formerly known as Future Farmers of America). The upbringing of most children is heavily steeped in the aura of animals, from cartoons and songs to fables and toys. Animals adorn their clothing, their bedroom walls, their baths, and even their eating utensils. Real animals, too, are a powerful presence; parents take their children to zoos and marine parks and often bring pets into the home specifically to make kids happy.

The ag industry capitalizes on this affinity, encouraging kids to raise cows, sheep, pigs, goats and other animals, principally through 4-H's Youth Livestock Program and the FFA's Supervised Agricultural Experience. In both of these programs, children care for animals for several months or even a year. After bonding deeply with their animal, the child must sell them for slaughter. It's often a visceral gut punch for kids.

A typical example is Dalton Carpenter, who raised two lambs, named Pork and Beans, in a 4-H program when he was eight. Six months later, he was showing Beans at Colorado's Douglas County Fair, where she was sold for US$2,100. An image of Dalton, tears streaming down his face as he was saying goodbye to Beans, went viral. "It was hard," Dalton said later. "Because I raised her. I took care of her. And then she was gone."[8]

Invariably, parents of children involved in youth ag programs will gush about how proud they are of their son or daughter for overcoming their emotional attachment and learning one of life's "important lessons," which is that not only does the food we eat come from animals, but these animals were put on Earth for humans to use.

This justification for eating animals is known as the doctrine of dominionism, which is based on the Judeo-Christian belief that humans shall "have dominion over the fish of the sea and the birds in the sky and over every living creature that moves on the ground" – at least according to the biblical Book of Genesis. In 2010, the journal *Animals and Society* published a study on the 4-H Youth Livestock Program, finding it to be "an apprenticeship in which children learn to do cognitive emotion work, use distancing mechanisms, and create a 'redemption' narrative to cope with contradictory ethical and emotional experiences."[9]

The key words there are "cognitive emotion work," which is a fancy way of saying the kids are taught not to become attached to animals who are destined to be killed. For example, 4-H apprentices eventually learn not to name their animals. Why? Because giving a farmed animal a name turns them into an individual in the eyes and hearts of children. Family members have names. Friends have names. Pets have names. Kids see that a calf or lamb or pig will come when their name is called – that these animals are no different than a dog or cat or rabbit – and things get complicated. Thus, by not naming an animal, it's easier to emotionally distance themselves from someone they know will soon die. (The 2010 study found that no child over the age of 15 named the animals they were raising, while every child under 15 readily told researchers the names of their animals.)

The "redemption" narrative mentioned in the 4-H study refers to the practice of placing a dollar value on farmed animals. By viewing these animals as a commodity – and putting the money they earn into a college fund, for instance – children learn to further distance themselves from the animals, regarding their relationship with them as a means to an end and helping to reduce whatever emotional conflict they might feel.

"Honoring" Animals Used for Food

We cannot examine the intersection of humans, animals, and spirituality without touching on the practice of thanking an animal for their "sacrifice" before eating them. Such a custom dates back thousands of years, and it remains a popular ritual among some meat-eaters, who claim to "honor" the chicken, pig, cow, or other farmed animal for giving their life, as if the animal had some choice in the matter and decided to bestow a gift upon hungry humans. While such a magnanimous act may have a place in mythology, it's really rooted in a person's desire to rid themselves of guilt and the responsibility that accompanies animal consumption, and a number of otherwise spiritually minded educators are happy to carve an ethical exception for their followers. As one author and yoga teacher put it, "When eating flesh, it requires a level of honoring and gratitude."[10]

While I suppose that attitude and its attendant air of ostensible thoughtfulness implies the person gives more consideration to where their food comes from than the average consumer, I don't believe it's an adequate defense for their role in taking another's life. And make no mistake: it *is* a defense. I think a lot of meat-eaters try to convince themselves – using whatever reasoning is at hand – that their taste for animal flesh is an acceptable habit.

If we truly wish to honor another species, by far the most compassionate practice is to acknowledge their desire and right to be left alone.

Sadly, a lot of religious leaders, including so-called "enlightened masters," eat animals. Many of them say they do so because that's how they grew up and they see no reason to change. At an event in support of a free Tibet, I had a conservation with one of the Dalai Lama's physicians, who told me he advised His Holiness to eat meat for his health, which I understand he does once or twice a week. (An especially disappointing practice for such a high-placed Buddhist leader.)

With so many of the world's religious traditions supposedly focused on compassion and nonviolence, it makes sense to wonder how eating animals – or *not* eating them – affects you.

Let me share an example from personal experience. In the fall of 1992, I found myself living with a Buddhist family in the Himalayas of India. I consider myself to be a spiritual person, and like most people, I grew up consuming animals. But in

Ladakh, where I lived for two months, almost everything I ate came from the garden of the house I was staying in (the family didn't grow rice, which had to be purchased in town). My diet was based on fresh vegetables and fruits.

After a few weeks, I began noticing how different I felt. It was a feeling perhaps best described as a lightness, as if the weight of the world I had carried with me for so many years was gradually lifted. I also felt a powerful connection to both the Earth and a divine presence. Granted, I could have been experiencing the influence of many hours spent in Ladakhi monasteries and temples – meditation and sandalwood incense can have that effect on you – but I knew it was something more than that. It was the beginning of my path to veganism.

One of the things that not eating animals rid me of was the responsibility I felt for taking a life. Although I didn't wield the knife, whenever I'd eaten animals, I still felt guilty, and that was one reason I felt lighter. I believe that any thoughtful person who consumes animals struggles with this same guilt, and making the switch to vegan foods is a major step on the path to peace.

Everyone is on their own path, of course, and none of us is perfect. Can you practice eco-spirituality (or *any* kind of spirituality) and eat animals? I suppose you can. But perhaps the better question is, will eating animals – will participating in violence – hinder your spiritual growth? In the case of eco-spirituality, which is built upon a deep connection with nature, I would argue that the answer is yes.

Endnotes

1. https://faunalytics.org/global-animal-slaughter-statistics-and-charts/
2. William H. Williams, *Delmarva's Chicken Industry: 75 Years of Progress* (Delmarva Poultry Industry), 1998, pages 11–13.
3. https://www.nationalchickencouncil.org/about-the-industry/statistics/u-s-broiler-performance/

4. Peter Singer, "Factory farming: A moral issue," *The Minnesota Daily*, March 22, 2006, https://mndaily.com/248334/opinion/factory-farming-moral-issue/

5. P.R. Shukla, J. Skea, E. Calvo Buendia, "Climate Change and Land: an IPCC special report on climate change, desertification, land degradation, sustainable land management, food security, and greenhouse gas fluxes in terrestrial ecosystems," IPCC, 2019, https://www.ipcc.ch/srccl/

6. K.A. Johnson and D.E. Johnson, "Methane emissions from cattle," *Journal of Animal Science*, Volume 73, Number 8, August 1995, https://pubmed.ncbi.nlm.nih.gov/8567486/

7. "Why Methane Matters," United Nations, https://unfccc.int/news/new-methane-signs-underline-urgency-to-reverse-emissions

8. Tomas Hoppough, "Picture of Franktown 8-year-old selling lamb at Douglas County Fair goes viral," ABC-TV Denver, August 10, 2018, https://www.thedenverchannel.com/news/trending/picture-of-franktown-8-year-old-selling-lamb-goes-viral

9. Colter Ellis and Leslie Irvine, "Reproducing Dominion: Emotional Apprenticeship in the 4-H Youth Livestock Program," *Society and Animals*, Volume 18, 2010, pages 21–39, https://www.animalsandsociety.org/wp-content/uploads/2016/04/ellis.pdf

10. Tresca Weinstein, "How to Be a Conscious and Responsible Omnivore," Sonima.com, March 13, 2015, https://www.sonima.com/food/eating-meat/

Chapter 2

Animals in Captivity

The human race is challenged more than ever before to demonstrate our mastery – not over nature but of ourselves. – Rachel Carson

Most people will never have the experience of seeing an elephant in their native habitat. Those who do see one of these remarkable beings in person will likely observe them in a zoo or perhaps a circus, although elephants in circuses are becoming less common.

I raise this point because for many of us, being near an elephant or a gorilla or a tiger or a whale or any other charismatic megafauna (large animals with wide appeal) is somewhere on the spectrum of the human–animal relationship. We've long been fascinated by the strength and beauty of these animals, and for nearly as long we've found ways to make them available to us for convenient viewing.

Ancient cultures, who regarded wild animals as an integral part of the natural world, sought to keep live animals in collections, though these proto zoos were generally in the hands of royalty and wealthy classes.

Among the first societies to keep animals in captivity were the Egyptians, which may have done so for spiritual or religious reasons. There is evidence that in ancient Egypt, antelopes, baboons, cheetahs, cranes, falcons, hyenas, and storks were kept, and some of these animals were considered sacred.[1] The baboon, for instance, was thought to be one manifestation of the moon god Thoth, the god of writing and knowledge.[2]

Kings in Assyria, Babylonia, and Sumeria were proud of their animal "collections," which included camels, elephants, lions, monkeys, and other species intended to impress foreign dignitaries and symbolize the king's wealth, power, and authority. Under their reigns, monarchs created elaborate gardens and parks to house animals in captivity, and some of them resembled their natural counterparts. Sennacherib, for instance, king of the Neo-Assyrian Empire from 705 B.C.E. to 681 B.C.E., so admired a marsh environment in southern Babylonia that he had it recreated and populated with animals and plants imported from the actual swamp from across the border.[3]

The zoo as we know it, however – with paying customers coming in to gawk at animals in captivity – is a much more recent creation. Most historians consider Vienna's Tiergarten Schönbrunn to be the world's oldest zoo, established in 1752 and then opened to the public in 1765. The next few decades saw zoos founded in Madrid and Paris. In the first half of the nineteenth century, zoos in London, Dublin, Melbourne, and several cities in Germany were attracting people to see their animal "collections." The premise of zoos during this time was that they could bring extraordinary natural wonders to an audience that would not ordinarily have any knowledge of or access to them.

Moreover, the growing popularity of zoos coincided with the gradual urbanization of the landscape and the removal of large animals from cities. With the Industrial Revolution, for instance, the power of the internal combustion engine was able to replace horses and mules, who had been used for pulling streetcars, hauling wagons, and other forced labor. "Public zoos came into existence at the beginning of the period which was to see the disappearance of animals from daily life," wrote the English author and critic John Berger. "The zoo to which people go to meet animals, to observe them, to see them, is, in fact, a monument to the impossibility of such encounters. Modern zoos are an epitaph to a relationship which was as old as man."[4]

That relationship was always in a state of flux, with some animal species finding favor among humans and other species regarded more for what benefit could be derived from them.

By the Victorian Era, it seems, the benefit derived from many wild animals – they were also called "exotic animals" – was as entertainment. And thus the human–animal relationship took on another wrinkle of complication.

In the modern defense of zoos, entertainment is generally regarded as one of the four key benefits, along with education, conservation, and scientific research. Entertainment was a major reason for the establishment of the first zoos, and most people continue to view a day at the zoo as a form of amusement. But entertainment has become a morally indefensible argument for keeping animals in captivity.

With zoos becoming more controversial in recent decades – often equated with human prisons – zoo and aquarium officials have tried to pivot their emphasis from entertainment to conservation, research, and education. In the face of climate change and rapidly disappearing habitats, they claim, captivity offers protection for endangered species while also teaching the public about animals and providing scientists with opportunities to study wild animals up close.

Education is probably the justification most often touted by zoos and aquaria for keeping animals in captivity, and yet studies continue to demonstrate that visitors learn little or nothing at all – or even have a negative learning experience. A study of 2,839 visitors (ages 7 to 15) to the London Zoo published in 2014, for example, found that only 38 percent of children had positive learning outcomes, while 62 percent either learned nothing at the zoo or had a negative learning experience in which they came out with a misunderstanding of animals and their habitats.[5]

Likewise, the idea that seeing animals in an aquarium or marine park is educational has been roundly denounced by a number of scientists. Most notable among these captivity critics is Dr. Naomi Rose, a cetacean biologist with the US-based Animal Welfare Institute and a member of the International Whaling Commission Scientific Committee. In 2017, Dr. Rose addressed a

Canadian Senate committee on fisheries and oceans, which was meeting to hear debate on a bill to end the practice of keeping whales, dolphins, and porpoises in captivity and protect them from suffering the psychological and physical injuries caused by spending their lives in a tiny tank.

Dr. Rose told the committee that almost everything people hear about animals once inside the gates of aquaria and marine parks is incorrect. "When a child sees a show, they don't see reality," she said. "They're seeing a facade. Something that is false. I find it really disturbing." Visitors have the false impression that everything is fine with the whales and dolphins, she added, because they are swimming and jumping. "Zoos and aquariums are making it worse for these species because they pretty much have to lie to the public to make it seem okay that these animals are in this box of water."

Conservative Senator Donald Plett took issue with Dr. Rose's characterization of marine mammals in captivity, citing a report on Kiska, a female orca taken from the wild in 1979 and now passing her days and nights at Marineland Ontario. Plett said the report determined Kiska to be stress-free and psychologically fit. "Kiska is completely abnormal," Dr. Rose replied. "I'm a killer whale biologist. I've spent hours watching her and there is nothing about her that teaches a child an accurate picture of killer whales. I actually think Kiska is hampering our ability to show people what these animals need."

Senator Plett then held up a photo he took of Kiska at the pool surface, with her mouth open, waiting to be fed. "I've met her," he said. "She looked pretty normal to me, smiling when I touched her."

"They smile even when they're dead," Dr. Rose responded. "That photograph is of a stance you never see in the wild. Head out of the water, that 'smile' – she's begging for food. Food comes from the sky in captivity."[6] (Canada's House of Commons passed the so-called "Free Willy" bill in 2019.)

In an attempt to refute such criticism, in 2007 the American Zoo and Aquarium Association (AZA) released a study that was widely regarded as the first direct evidence that visits to zoos and aquaria produce long-term positive effects on people's attitudes toward animals. An examination led by researchers at Emory University, however, found the AZA study to be deeply flawed. The authors concluded that "to date there is no compelling or even particularly suggestive evidence for the claim that zoos and aquariums promote attitude change, education, and interest in conservation in visitors."[7]

In his essay "Zoos Revisited," Dale Jamieson, Professor of Environmental Studies and Philosophy at New York University, asks if there is a presumption against keeping animals in captivity, and then argues that the answer is yes: "Keeping animals in captivity usually involves restricting their liberty in ways that deny them many goods including gathering their own food, developing their own social orders, and generally behaving in ways that are natural to them. In the case of many animals, captivity also involves removing them from their native habitats and conditions. If animals have any moral standing at all, then it is plausible to suppose that depriving them of liberty is presumptively wrong, since an interest in liberty is central to most morally significant creatures."[8]

Such restriction in an animal's liberty routinely results in highly repetitive, functionless behavior, such as pacing back and forth, head bobbing, bar biting, excessive grooming, or even self-harm. It's a displayed common stereotypic behavior (sometimes called "zoochosis" — psychosis caused by captivity) often seen in animals who are bored, frustrated, lonely, and depressed. In the mid-1990s, Gus, a polar bear in New York's Central Park Zoo obsessively swam figure eights in his small pool, 12 hours a day, every day. Gus' enclosure was just 5,000 square feet — less than .00009 percent of what his range in the Arctic would be. When the zoo spent $25,000 on an animal behaviorist, Gus "the bipolar bear" became a national punchline.

Two decades later, when young visitors to the Himeji City Zoo in Japan would ask their parents why Himeko the elephant was continuously swaying and bobbing her head, many parents would say she was "dancing." No, she was not dancing. Himeko, who died in 2020, compulsively moved to help cope with the stress of spending 26 years alone in a habitat that could never meet her physical and emotional needs. The zoo knew better, of course, and ignored the voices of animal advocates who asked that Himeko be freed from her captive isolation.

Perhaps predictably, rather than give animals in captivity the freedom they deserve, zoo officials now treat stressed animals with a variety of pharmaceuticals intended to manage anxiety. "At every zoo where I spoke to someone, a psychopharmaceutical had been tried," says Laurel Braitman, author of *Animal Madness*. She says that drugs are an attractive option for zoos because "they are a hell of a lot less expensive than re-doing your $2 million exhibit or getting rid of that problem creature." But it's not a practice that zoos are proud of, since "finding out that the gorillas, badgers, giraffes, belugas, or wallabies on the other side of the glass are taking Valium, Prozac, or antipsychotics to deal with their lives as display animals is not exactly heartwarming news."[10]

Zoos have tried other methods for improving the lives of animals under their control. Moats eventually replaced bars in many enclosures, which was more aesthetically pleasing while bringing the animals closer to the public. Attention has also been paid to the environment of the enclosure, with attempts to create something akin to the animal's "natural" habitat. Trees, water features, and artificial rocks formed from concrete are often added to approximate what animals experience in the wild.

Yet the real motivation behind creating faux-habitats for animals in captivity isn't to make the animals happier – it's a profit-motivated sleight of hand designed to assuage any guilt we might feel about plunking down our hard-earned money to see animals who, let's face it, are merely live exhibits. It's no secret that zoos are for people, not for animals, and I imagine the simulated environments built for these animals probably feel about as authentic to them as living in a small plastic doll house would for humans.

What zoos *have* kept secret, or tried to, is the fate of their so-called "surplus" animals. As much as zoos maintain that they are institutions of conservation and education, they are still motivated by the balance sheet, and that often means being able to feature new animals who keep visitors coming through the turnstiles. Once an animal outgrows their usefulness, however, zoos are faced with what to do with them. One solution was to transfer the animal to a dealer, who would then sell them to a hunting ranch, roadside zoo, circus, research lab, or some other enterprise, though this practice has largely declined thanks to a wave of bad publicity in recent decades.

A "surplus" animal is more likely to be "warehoused": kept in a back-of-the-house section of the zoo where multiple animals are locked away in cages, never to be seen by visitors.[11]

A more common and controversial practice among zoos, however, is to kill the animal. Exact figures on how many animals are killed by zoos are not available, but the European Association of Zoos and Aquaria (EAZA) estimates that their 340 member zoos kill somewhere between 3,000 and 5,000 animals a year.[12] And that's just zoos in Europe that happen to belong to the Amsterdam-based EAZA organization. "As morally reprehensible as the practice of killing surplus animals seems, it's a reality and part of business as usual for many zoos," wrote animal advocate Marc Bekoff in an article for Salon.com.[13]

While the killing of zoo animals is generally kept quiet for fear of offending the public, Danish zookeepers have the opposite attitude. The Copenhagen Zoo, for instance, was not at all shy about shooting a healthy, 18-month-old giraffe named

Marius in 2014, dissecting him, and then feeding his remains to lions. Marius' crime? His genes were over-represented in the captive population within EAZA zoos, making him unsuitable for breeding.[14] When the same zoo killed and then dissected a young lion in front a family audience a month before shooting Marius, the dismemberment was staged as part of a weekend-long event called "Animals Inside Out."[15]

(In addition to their record of animal abuse, zoos have been linked to shocking racism. Perhaps the most famous example is the Bronx Zoo, which in 1906 put an African "pygmy" named Ota Benga – who had been kidnapped from his home in Congo and taken to the US – on display alongside apes in their Monkey House. After 114 years of denying they did anything wrong, the Bronx Zoo apologized in 2020.[16])

Many of the same sorts of concerns for animal welfare that are directed at zoos are also leveled at other forms of captivity, especially circuses.

Both of these institutions rely on two fundamental human aspirations: the desire for amusement and the longing to connect with nature – even if it means that nature has been all but removed from the experience. In the case of circuses, customers are no doubt more motivated by wanting to be *entertained* by "exotic" animals than by simply being near them, but it's surprising how often circuses have claimed that they offer educational value.

Like zoos, circuses have centuries-old roots – in ancient Rome, for example, a circus (Latin for "circle") was an arena built for mass entertainments like chariot races and gladiator fights – but the elements we know them for today, such as animals trained to perform tricks beneath a large canvas tent, didn't become common until the nineteenth century.[17] Traveling as they did from city to city, circuses were once big events that everyone wanted to witness. Shops often closed their doors for the day and schools cancelled classes.[18] Suddenly, not only were all the most popular animals from a zoo – elephants, bears, tigers, zebras, lions, monkeys, seals, and more – right in town, but they would dance, jump through flaming hoops, balance on balls, ride bicycles, toot horns, and demonstrate other remarkable feats.

Training animals to perform these tricks involves physical punishment, deprivation, fear, and submission. An in-depth investigation by the nonprofit Animal Defenders International (ADI) found that animal abuse is part of the working culture in circuses throughout the US, UK, Europe, and South America. According to their report, animals are frequently beaten, kicked, stabbed, and whipped to make them obey. Among ADI's other tragic findings about animals in circuses: elephants spend 58 to 98 percent of their time chained by at least one leg, and generally both a front and hind leg; tigers and lions spend between 75 and 99 percent of their time in severely cramped cages on the backs of trailers; horses and ponies spend up to 96 percent of their time tied with short ropes in stalls, or tethered to trailers; and extended periods being tied up, chained, or caged with no freedom of movement results in abnormal behaviors that indicate these animals are suffering as a result of a poor environment and welfare provision.[19]

Such cruelty is a major reason that cities, states, and countries are limiting or banning the use of animals in circuses. Austria, Belgium, Bolivia, Columbia, Costa Rica, Denmark, England, Greece, Guatemala, India, Ireland, Mexico, Netherlands, Norway, Scotland, and Wales are just some of the countries that have prohibited the use of wild animals. Progress in the United States has been slow, but California, Hawaii, and New Jersey have passed bans on using wild animals, and others are sure to follow.

The tragic irony of zoos, circuses, and aquaria is that many people who visit these institutions do indeed want to connect with animals, but captivity does not allow for this – at least not in any significant way. In large part that is because we are both at a disadvantage. The animal in captivity is merely surviving day to day, an existence that is but a poor imitation of their life in the natural world. They are not greeting us on equal footing, which would seem to be a critical element of any meaningful bond between us. And we are hindered because we can only justify "conquering" nature and putting her on display if we regard as animals as the "other." The human–animal connection is lost, and we are to blame.

Endnotes

1. Stephen St. C. Bostock, *Zoos and Animal Rights: The Ethics of Keeping Animals* (Routledge, 1993).
2. "Sacred animals of ancient Egypt," Reading Museum, May 15, 2020, https://www.readingmuseum.org.uk/blog/sacred-animals-ancient-egypt
3. Vernon N. Kisling, Jr., "Ancient Collections and Menageries," from *Zoo and Aquarium History Ancient Animal Collections To Zoological Gardens*, edited by Vernon N. Kisling, Jr. (CRC Press, 2000), pp. 10–11.
4. John Berger, *Why Look at Animals?* (Penguin Books, 2009), p. 15.
5. Eric Jensen, "Evaluating Children's Conservation Biology Learning at the Zoo," *Conservation Biology*, 2014, Volume 28, Number 4.
6. Holly Lake, "No evidence zoos and aquariums foster education or conservation, committee told," IPolitics.ca, April 5, 2017, https://ipolitics.ca/2017/04/05/no-evidence-zoos-and-aquariums-foster-education-or-conservation-committee-told/
7. Lori Marino, Scott O. Lilienfeld, et al., "Do zoos and aquariums promote attitude change in visitors? A critical evaluation of the American zoo and aquarium study," *Society & Animals*, 2010, Volume 18, Number 2, https://www.wellbeingintlstudiesrepository.org/acwp_zoae/8/
8. Dale Jamieson, "Zoos Revisited," from *Morality's Progress:*

Essays on Humans, Other Animals, and the Rest of Nature by Dale Jamieson (Clarendon Press, 2002), p. 179.

9. Laurel Braitman, "Even the Gorillas and Bears in Our Zoos Are Hooked on Prozac," Wired.com, July 15, 2014, https://www.wired.com/2014/07/animal-madness-laurel-braitman/

10. Laura Smith, "Zoos Drive Animals Crazy," Slate, June 20, 2014, https://slate.com/technology/2014/06/animal-madness-zoochosis-stereotypic-behavior-and-problems-with-zoos.html

11. Scott Carter and Ron Kagen, "Management of 'Surplus' Animals," from *Wild Animals in Captivity: Principles & Techniques for Zoo Management,* Second Edition, edited by Devra G. Kleiman, Katerina V. Thompson, and Charlotte Kirk Baer (University of Chicago Press, 2012), p. 265.

12. Hannah Barnes, "How many healthy animals do zoos put down?" BBC News, February 27, 2014, https://www.bbc.com/news/magazine-26356099

13. Dr. Marc Bekoff, "Zoothanasia: the cruel practice of killing healthy zoo animals," Salon.com, February 3, 2018, https://www.salon.com/2018/02/03/zoothanasia-the-cruel-practice-of-killing-healthy-zoo-animals_partner/

14. Paul Rincon, "Why did Copenhagen Zoo kill its giraffe?" BBC News, February 10, 2014, https://www.bbc.com/news/science-environment-26118748

15. Ian Parker, "Killing Animals at the Zoo," *The New Yorker*, January 16, 2017, https://www.newyorker.com/magazine/2017/01/16/killing-animals-at-the-zoo

16. Pamela Newkirk, "Caged Congolese teen: Why a zoo took 114 years to apologize," BBC, August 27, 2020, https://www.bbc.com/news/world-africa-53917733

17. Janet M. Davis, "America's Big Circus Spectacular Has a Long and Cherished History," Smithsonianmag.com, March 22, 2017, https://www.smithsonianmag.com/history/americas-big-circus-spectacular-has-long-and-cherished-

history-180962621/

18. Janet M. Davis, *The Circus Age: Culture & Society Under the American Big Top* (University of North Carolina Press, 2002), p. 2.
19. Animal Defenders International, *Animals in Traveling Circuses: The Science on Suffering*, July 14, 2008, www.ad-international.org/animals_in_entertainment/go.php?id=1368

Chapter 3

Animals in Labs

Human beings destroy their ecology at the same time that they destroy each other From that perspective, healing our society goes hand in hand with healing our personal, elemental connection with the phenomenal world. – Chögyam Trungpa

There is arguably no human–animal relationship more complicated than the use of animals in biomedical research, product testing, and education. That is because, from the point of view of the experimenters, animals are both like humans and not like humans: they share so many physical characteristics with humans as to justify using them as biological substitutes for us, and yet they are different enough from humans to rationalize their use in unspeakable ways.

The scientists' duplicitous view of animals as both like us and not like us is at best hypocrisy and at worst malpractice, since non-human species are so physically unlike us that they do not react the way a human would to many of the drugs tested on them. In 1998, Dr. Richard Klausner, then director of the National Cancer Institute in the United States, put it this way: "The history of cancer research has been a history of curing cancer in the mouse. We have cured mice of cancer for decades – and it simply didn't work in humans."[1]

In a 2015 interview, another cancer expert, oncologist Azra Raza, agreed that mice do not mimic human disease well and are essentially worthless for drug development. "It's very clear that if we are to improve cancer therapy, we have to study human cancer cells," she said. "But in my opinion too many eminent laboratories and illustrious researchers have devoted entire lives to studying malignant diseases in mouse models. And they are the ones reviewing each other's grants and deciding where money gets spent."[2]

Dr. Raza's point about grants is important, and it's one of the essential reasons animal testing continues, even in the face of humane options. "Grant money is the mainstay of research university budgets, so there is a huge financial incentive to conduct federally funded research on animals, since the university gets a big cut of the money from all grants awarded to its faculty members," says Lawrence Hansen, MD, a professor of neuroscience and pathology at the University of California–San Diego, and one of the medical community's most outspoken critics of animal research.[3]

Another physician explains: "If I get a million-dollar grant to study osteoporosis in elderly women, the university where I'm employed will get none of that money. But if I get a million-dollar grant to study osteoporosis in mice, the university gets roughly fifty percent of that. So there's no real mystery here about what the motivating factor is from the university's perspective."[4]

Let's take a closer look at the three main categories of animal testing.

Biomedical Research

Biomedical research is by far the largest category. Here animals are used as models of people to study human health, disease, and injury. This category also includes testing drugs to determine their toxicity (how poisonous they are). Research generally leads to clinical trials using humans.

The history of using animals for biomedical research can be traced back to at least the fifth century BCE, when the Greek scientist Alcmaeon of Crotona studied the optic nerve by dissecting the eyes of live dogs.[5] Early researchers also studied human cadavers, but by the time of the physician Galen in the second century CE, the Church had prohibited autopsies, so he acquired goats, pigs, and monkeys from North Africa to experiment on, thus securing his place in history as the father of vivisection.[6] Galen's influence spread throughout medieval Europe as scientists regarded the Roman physician's conclusions – including dangerous blunders about the heart and blood vessels – as unassailable.

In the seventeenth century, vivisectors embraced the teachings of René Descartes, whose philosophy, known as Cartesianism, portrayed animals as soulless, unthinking machines.[7] Some Cartesians even claimed that animals felt no pain.[8] Consequently, researchers looked upon live animals as no morally different than such inanimate objects as a chair or microscope and thus felt free to carry out the cruelest experiments imaginable. The scientist Robert Hooke, for instance, performed one procedure before the Royal Society of London in 1667 in which he opened a live dog's chest by cutting away the ribs and diaphragm to expose the lungs and heart. He then severed the windpipe and attached it to the nose of a bellows pump, which he used to force air into the dog's lungs. To refute the commonly-held belief that the lungs produced blood circulation, Hooke poked the animal's lungs full of holes with a penknife and noted how air flowed through the punctures. This went on for an hour, with Hooke even cutting out a piece of one of the dog's lungs.[9] Hooke observed that when he stopped pumping the bellows, "the Dog would immediately fall into Dying convulsive fits" but could be revived again with "a blast of fresh Air."[10]

More than three and a half centuries later, the use of animals in biomedical research is more entrenched than ever, with animal research now a major component of the global US$270-billion, government-subsidized biomedical industry.[11] Researchers divide their argument for studying animals into four justifications: to improve humanity's understanding of biology; to serve as models in the study of diseases; to develop and test potential treatments; and to protect the safety of humans, animals, and the environment. In these pursuits, each year researchers subject millions of mice, fishes, rabbits, rats, guinea pigs, dogs, hamsters, pigs, sheep, chimpanzees, cats, and other species to painful studies that they hope will lead to a cure for a disease or provide some other benefit to humans. In almost every case, the animal dies during or is killed after the experiment.

Product Testing

Product testing involves performing toxicity tests on animals to assess the possible effect of pesticides, cosmetics, cleansers, food additives, tobacco, and a broad assortment of industrial and consumer goods on humans and the environment. Common tests measure the level of skin irritancy and eye tissue damage a substance causes.

Companies have made it a standard practice to conduct whatever toxicological trials they believe are appropriate to demonstrate the safety of their products. As a result, animals are subjected to a wide range of painful "safety tests" in which corrosive chemicals are dripped into their eyes, toxic compounds already known to be fatal to humans are pumped into their stomachs, caustic irritants are rubbed into their skin, or an assortment of other unspeakable tortures that result in a painful death.

Thanks to concern for animal welfare, there has been a wave of reform on product testing, and many countries, including the UK, New Zealand, Israel, and members of the European Union, have banned cosmetics testing on animals. Some countries, such as Australia, have banned using animals for cosmetics testing, but chemicals that are intended for use in cosmetics may still be tested on them provided the purpose for the testing is justified by a non-cosmetic purpose (for example, a chemical ingredient intended to be used in both a shampoo product *and* a laundry detergent). For now, though, these bans only concern cosmetics – pesticides, cleansers, and other household products are not covered.

In the United States, not even a ban on cosmetics testing has yet to be passed. Nor is testing products on animals required by US law.[12] The most common product tests performed on animals in the US are the LD50 test, the Draize Eye Irritancy Test, and the Draize Skin Irritancy Test.

The LD50 Test

The Lethal Dose 50 Percent test, or LD50, measures how much of a tested chemical it takes to kill half the animals it's administered to within a specified time period, although the objective is to set safe toxicity levels for human consumers. Products tested using LD50 range from pesticides and shampoos to drugs and cosmetics. The victims of LD50 testing are typically dogs and rats, but they might also be mice, rabbits, monkeys, guinea pigs, fish, and birds.[13] Incremental doses of a substance, measured in milligrams per kilogram of body weight, are injected, applied to the skin or eyes, introduced into the lungs, or force-fed into a group of subjects until 50 percent of the animals are dead. The median lethal dose becomes that chemical's LD50. For example, an "LD50 oral" of 4.5 in dogs means that 50 of 100 dogs died after being fed 4.5 grams of a tested substance per kilogram of body weight. The lower the LD50 rating, the more toxic the substance.

The LD50 test was developed by J.W. Trevan, a British pharmacologist, in 1927 as a quality control for medications such as digitalis and insulin and has since become an international standard measurement of acute toxicity.[14] Tests may last anywhere from 14 days to six months, depending on the substance being measured and the species used. Before an animal dies, they may experience, among other symptoms, abdominal pain, internal bleeding, paralysis, convulsions, or bleeding from the nose, mouth, eyes, or rectum. A particularly gruesome demise awaits animals used to test the popular anti-wrinkle treatment Botox. In these LD50 tests, researchers inject the drug's active ingredient – a highly potent neurotoxin known as botulinum – into groups of mice. Botulinum toxin is the most poisonous known substance, often used as a biological weapon, and even a miniscule amount can kill a human. In the laboratory, mice suffer a slow and excruciating death by suffocation as their respiratory muscles become paralyzed.[15] All for a product that temporarily removes frown lines.

Animal advocates and scientists alike have criticized LD50 as cruel, outdated, and ineffective. LD50 tests offer no information that would help treat poisoning in humans (animal testing does not make toxic chemicals less deadly), nor do they address toxicity to organs.[16] One of the principle problems with LD50 is that it's a statistical expression of a substance's toxicity under *controlled conditions* – in other words, the tests cannot reliably predict risk because they cannot account for a wide variety of other factors, such as the environment or even the method of testing used (it is not uncommon for a force-fed chemical to result in disease, whereas injection of the same chemical does not). Moreover, there is no agreement on how to extrapolate animal test results to humans. Exacerbating this challenge is the fact that animal species respond to poison in different ways. For instance, rats and rabbits cannot vomit and thereby eliminate toxins from their bodies, while such a reaction is normal for people. In his critique of LD50, the Swiss toxicologist Gerhard Zbinden described the tests as little more than "a ritual mass execution of animals."[17]

The Draize Tests

Developed in 1944 by FDA toxicologist John H. Draize and his colleagues, the Draize tests attempt to evaluate the risks of exposure to cosmetics, cleansers, and other products. There are two such tests: the Draize Eye Irritancy Test and the Draize Skin Irritancy Test, both of which cause tremendous suffering to the animals used.

In the Draize test for eye irritancy, a liquid, granule, flake, or powdered substance is applied to one eye of a non-anesthetized rabbit. (Rabbits are considered ideal subjects for this test because of the way they produce tears, making it harder to dilute or eliminate the substance, though this fact alone would seem to put the test's applicability to humans in question.) If you've ever had a grain of sand or other foreign object in your eye – let alone a caustic chemical – you can imagine the misery the rabbit is made to suffer. Describing a common reaction before test subjects were held motionless in stocks, one researcher observed: "Animal holds eye shut urgently. May squeal, claw at eye, jump and try to escape."[18] Now during most of these procedures, which may last several days or even weeks, the rabbit's eyes are held open with clips.[19] Researchers then measure the level of tissue damage. In addition to causing intense pain, the tested compounds often leave the animals' eyes ulcerated, infected, swollen, and bleeding.[20] Whatever the results, the rabbit is killed once the test is complete.

In the Draize Skin Irritancy Test, technicians shave a section of the animal's fur (again, usually a rabbit, although guinea pigs, mice, rats, dogs, and cats are also used in this test) and abrade their skin by repeatedly applying and ripping off adhesive tape. A test substance is applied to the skin and the area is covered with a gauze pad and wrapped in plastic sheeting or rubber. The animal is then immobilized and the skin reaction is checked and given a score on the Draize scale after four, 24, and 72 hours.[21] An animal may be used up to six times for these tests before they are killed, and several victims are used simultaneously for each test.

Both Draize tests have been condemned as much for their accuracy as for their cruelty, even by the scientific community. A study comparing the use of rabbits and humans as subjects in eye irritancy tests found that the two species respond very differently to substances, concluding that using animals overestimates how the human eye will respond.[22] One researcher hired to experiment on animals, meanwhile, admitted the eye irritancy test is callous and pointless. "I felt numb – no, guilty," she said about applying a common toothpaste ingredient to the eye of a terrified rabbit. "It isn't as if the end justified the means. We weren't researching some cancer cure here. We were testing a well-known chemical that has been used in household products for more than 100 years."[23]

Meanwhile, humane alternatives for predicting how human eyes and skin will react to toxins are being developed. Examples include computer-based models of the eye and skin, three-dimensional models of the eye, and lab-grown tissues that have been engineered to mimic the human epidermis.[24]

Education

Education, the third major category of animal testing, includes animals used in training medical, veterinary, and other health professionals or in teaching basic biology, such as anatomy. Dissecting frogs in high school is a common example most of us are probably familiar with.

Using animals as teaching aids has a long and ignoble history, especially the practice of dissection, which entails methodically cutting up and observing organisms. Some of the earliest animal dissections were conducted not in laboratories but in theater settings as a means of learning anatomy and biology. It was understood that animals were a substitute for humans, and the vivisectors of ancient Greece – and their audience – assumed that the organs of, say, a dog were analogous to the physiology of a man or woman.[25] This tradition continues today, though with a twist: now it's the high school, undergraduate, graduate, veterinary, and medical students who do the dissecting, not the instructors.

Classroom Dissection

For the last several generations, science classrooms have been where people generally have their first direct exposure to animal research. It is here that many students – armed with a scalpel, forceps, scissors, and probes – have been expected to pin down and slice open the remains of an animal or insect and explore their anatomy. It's a hands-on experience that leads to the death of millions of animals every year and leaves countless pupils either traumatized or desensitized (or both).

Campuses across the United States began embracing dissection in the 1920s, but it was generally limited to college-level courses. That all changed in the 1950s and '60s with the Cold War. The Soviet Union launched the world's first satellite into space in 1957 and, feeling their education system was lacking the scientific rigor of other countries, the US responded by infusing schools with new curricula emphasizing technology and biology. A federal grant from the National Science Foundation in 1958 led to an initiative called Biological Sciences Curriculum Study (BSCS), which made animal dissection much more widespread in secondary education. Soon high school biology classrooms were filled with frogs, cats, earthworms, rats, fetal pigs, starfish, turtles, sharks, and grasshoppers.[26] Not all these animals were dead when they arrived at the student's table.

A major component of BSCS was frog pithing, which required the student to destroy the living animal's brain by inserting a sharp probe into the base of the skull. This doesn't necessarily lead to immediate death, but supposedly renders the animal insensible to pain.[27] In other words, a pithed frog may be completely aware of everything going on throughout a dissection. One former biology student recalls being surprised that a pithed frog survived for several days, his beating heart clearly visible through his open chest cavity.[28] Frog pithing is still practiced in classrooms around the world.

Although there has been a shift toward using more non-animal tools in the US, the majority of biology teachers still include dissection as part of their coursework.[29] Classroom dissection is waning in Great Britain, where school administrators are abandoning the practice out of respect for students' ethical concerns – and fears that they could injure each other with their scalpels.[30]

Dissection is not simply a US or European exercise, of course. It is mandatory in biology classes throughout Hong Kong, for example, as it is in much of the rest of Asia. A notable exception is India, where animal dissection for undergraduate and postgraduate students was banned in 2014.[31] Other education systems, such as Australia and South Africa, have not made dissection compulsory, but leave it to the teacher's discretion.

Numerous studies show that dissection exercises can cause students to experience stress and trauma.[32] Reactions to this range from impaired cognitive abilities (resulting in less learning) to a numbing of the student's emotional and ethical integrity.[33] This numbing often heralds a gradual transition in which the student goes from being reluctant about dissection to entirely desensitized about the procedure – even regarding the animal's remains as garbage.

Medical Schools

The good news is that as of 2016, no medical school in the US or Canada uses live animals to teach surgical skills. Unfortunately, these countries appear to be among the exceptions, as medical schools in many other countries persist in using live animals to practice emergency medical procedures, and although dissection is now used less to teach manual dexterity, it continues to be justified as a way to teach anatomical structure. The position of pro-vivisection groups is that studying living systems is essential to learning about the structure of the body. But exercises using live animals have shown no measurable advantage over modern teaching alternatives, such as computer training programs. Moreover, most surgery residents develop their technical skills not by operating on animals, but by performing procedures on human patients while under the supervision of experienced practitioners.[34]

Veterinary Schools

One of the most controversial practices in the training of veterinarians is to use live, healthy animals. Perhaps it makes sense that students learning veterinary medicine would hone their skills and knowledge using animals. But because the veterinary field is a natural choice for science-inclined individuals who genuinely care about the welfare of animals, many vet students experience a deeply troubling conflict. Consider that the student may be required to participate in so-called "dog labs" in which animals are subjected to repeated surgical procedures, including practice in sewing up incisions, slicing into skin to study wounds, and the removal of vital organs. These are "terminal surgeries," meaning the animals are euthanized afterward, though they may be used in multiple procedures.

Although many veterinary schools have been removing terminal surgeries from their curriculum and replacing them with humane alternatives such as inanimate models and computer simulations, it is still common to find students practicing on live animals who are typically sourced from local animal shelters.[35] A more encouraging trend is that most veterinary schools also work with animal rescue organizations that allow students to perform supervised spay and neuter services for homeless animals.[36]

Endnotes

1. Marlene Cimons, Josh Getlin, and Thomas H. Maugh II, "Cancer Drugs Face Long Road From Mice to Men," *Los Angeles Times*, May 6, 1998, https://www.latimes.com/archives/la-xpm-1998-may-06-mn-46795-story.html

2. "Mice Are Not Men," Human Toxicology Project Consortium, May 18, 2015, https://htpconsortium.

wordpress.com/2015/05/18/mice-are-not-men/

3. Mark Hawthorne, *Bleating Hearts: The Hidden World of Animal Suffering* (Changemakers Books, 2013), p. 147.

4. Mark Hawthorne, *Bleating Hearts: The Hidden World of Animal Suffering* (Changemakers Books, 2013), p. 148.

5. Stephanie Watson, *Animal Testing: Issues and Ethics* (The Rosen Publishing Group, Inc., 2009), p. 11.

6. C. Ray Greek and Jean Swingle Greek, *Sacred Cows and Golden Geese: The Human Cost of Experiments on Animals* (Continuum International Publishing Group, 2000), p. 23.

7. Roger S. Fouts and Deborah H. Fouts, "Chimpanzees' Use of Sign Language," from *The Great Ape Project: Equality Beyond Humanity*, edited by Paola Cavalieri and Peter Singer (St. Martin's Press, 1993), p. 30.

8. Margaret A. Boden, *Mind as Machine: A History of Cognitive Science*, Volume 1 (Oxford University Press, 2006), p. 72.

9. Wallace Shugg, "Humanitarian Attitudes in the Early Animal Experiments of the Royal Society," *Annals of Science*, Volume 24, 1968.

10. Niall Shanks and C. Ray Greek, *Animal Models in Light of Evolution* (BrownWalker Press, 2009), p. 49.

11. Justin Chakma, Gordon H. Sun, et al., "Asia's Ascent Global Trends in Biomedical R&D Expenditures," *New England Journal of Medicine*, Volume 370, Number 1, 2014.

12. The US Food, Drug, and Cosmetic Act of 1938 "does not specifically require the use of animals in testing cosmetics for safety, nor does the Act subject cosmetics to FDA premarket approval. However, the agency has consistently advised cosmetic manufacturers to employ whatever testing is appropriate and effective for substantiating the safety of their products." www.fda.gov/Cosmetics/ProductandIngredientSafety/ProductTesting/ucm072268.htm

13. Mark H. Bernstein, *Without a Tear: Our Tragic Relationship*

with Animals (University of Illinois Press, 2004), p. 132.

14. Nancy Heneson, "American Agencies Denounce LD50 Test," *New Scientist*, November 17, 1983.

15. Silke Bitz, "The Botulinum Neurotoxin LD50 Test – Problems and Solutions," *Altex*, Volume 27, Number 2, February 2010.

16. Stephen R. Kaufmann and Murray J. Cohen, "The Clinical Relevance of the LD50," *Veterinary and Human Toxicology*, Volume 29, Issue 1, February 1987.

17. Gerhard Zbinden, *Progress in Toxicology*, Volume 1 (Springer-Verlag, 1973), p. 23.

18. Peter Singer, *Animal Liberation* (HarperCollins, 2002), p. 54.

19. Jordan Curnutt, *Animals and the Law: A Sourcebook* (ABC-CLIO, Inc., 2001), p. 450.

20. Susan E. Davis and Margo DeMello, *Stories Rabbits Tell: A Natural and Cultural History of a Misunderstood Creature* (Lantern Books, 2003), p. 285.

21. Wanda M. Haschek, Colin G. Rousseaux, and Matthew A. Wallig, *Fundamentals of Toxicologic Pathology*, second edition (Academic Press, 2010), p. 157.

22. R. Roggeband, M. York, M. Pericoi, and W. Braun, "Eye Irritation Responses in Rabbit and Man after Single Applications of Equal Volumes of Undiluted Model Liquid Detergent Products," *Food and Chemical Toxicology*, Volume 38, Issue 8, August 2000.

23. Steve Boggan, "Eight Million Animals Face Death to Test Your Toothpaste and Washing-up Liquid," *Daily Mail*, July 29, 2011.

24. Miri Lee, Jee-Hyun Hwang, and Kyung-Min Lim, "Alternatives to *In Vivo* Draize Rabbit Eye and Skin Irritation Tests with a Focus on 3D Reconstructed Human Cornea-Like Epithelium and Epidermis Models," *Toxicological Research*, Volume 33, Number 3, July 2017, https://www.ncbi.nlm.nih.gov/pmc/articles/PMC5523559/

25. Lynette A. Hart, Mary W. Wood, and Benjamin L. Hart,

Why Dissection?: Animal Use in Education (Greenwood Press, 2008), p. 18.

26. Marvin B. Emmons, "Secondary and Elementary School Use of Live and Preserved Animals," from *Animals in Education: Use of Animals in High School Biology Classes and Science Fairs*, edited by Heather McGiffin and Nanice Brownley (The Institute for the Study of Animal Problems, 1980), pp. 43–46.

27. Robert Amitrano and Gerard J. Tortora, *Laboratory Exercises in Anatomy and Physiology with Cat Dissections*, 8th edition (Thomson Brooks/Cole, 2007), p. 149.

28. Marcy C. Phipps, RN, CCRN, "The Soul on the Head of a Pin," *American Journal of Nursing*, Volume 110, Issue 5, May 2010.

29. Pamela Osenkowski, Che Green, et al., "Evaluation of Educator & Student Use of & Attitudes Toward Dissection & Dissection Alternatives," *The American Biology Teacher*, Volume 77, Issue 5, 2015, https://online.ucpress.edu/abt/article/77/5/340/18735/Evaluation-of-Educator-amp-Student-Use-of-amp

30. Heidi Blake, "Schools Abandon Dissection in Biology Lessons over Health and Safety Fears," *The Telegraph*, May 3, 2010.

31. Sruthy Susan Ullas, "Animal dissection banned in colleges," *The Times of India*, August 7, 2014, https://timesofindia.indiatimes.com/city/bengaluru/animal-dissection-banned-in-colleges/articleshow/39784719.cms

32. For examples see Paul F. Cunningham, "Animals in Psychology Education and Student Choice," *Society & Animals*, Volume 8, Number 2, 2000, and S. Plous, "Attitudes Toward the Use of Animals in Psychological Research and Education," *American Psychologist*, Volume 51, Number 11, November 1996.

33. Theodora Capaldo, "The Psychological Effects on Students of Using Animals in Ways that They See as Ethically, Morally

or Religiously Wrong," *Alternatives to Laboratory Animals*, Volume 32, June 2004.

34. R.W. Samsel, G.A. Schmidt, J.B. Hall, L.D.H. Wood, S.G. Shroff, and P.T. Schumacher, "Cardiovascular Physiology Teaching: Computer Simulations versus Animal Demonstrations," *American Journal of Physiology*, June 1994.

35. Cathy Barnette, "How and Why Are Shelter Pets Used in Vet Schools?" VetPrep.com, October 19, 2020, https://blog.vetprep.com/how-and-why-are-shelter-pets-used-in-vet-schools

36. Susan Krebsbach, DVM, "Vet Student Instrumental in Ending Terminal Surgeries," Humane Society Veterinary Medical Association, 2018, https://www.hsvma.org/vet_student_instrumental_in_ending_terminal_surgeries#.YQL1L-1lCb-

Chapter 4

Animals for Sport

There is no religion without love, and people may talk as much as
they like about their religion, but if it does not teach them to be good
and kind to beasts as well as man, it is all a sham – Anna Sewell

In considering the vast scope of human–animal relationships, the use of animals for sport represents a particular contradiction, as it often reflects humanity's attempt to conquer or subdue animals rather than foster any sort of meaningful connection with them. We can see this especially in blood sports such as bullfighting and in recreational hunting, where the objective is to demonstrate domination over an animal. Even in an apparently innocuous pastime like horseback riding, it is the human who has complete control over every aspect of the so-called sport, from how much weight the horse will be burdened with to when, where, and even how fast the two of them travel. People who own horses may profess deep affection for these animals, but ultimately the horse's back was never intended to serve as a seat for humans.

Undoubtedly one reason people love riding on horseback is that no human could ever run as fast as a healthy horse, and people seem to love the thrill of speed. Indeed, racing is one of the most popular forms of animal-related sport, and both horse racing and horse-drawn chariot racing were part of the ancient Olympic Games nearly 3,000 years ago.[1]

Animal races today include not only well-known contests such as horse racing, greyhound racing, and pigeon racing, but also ostrich racing, camel racing, hamster racing, and buffalo racing. The Australians seem to have a singular penchant for creating animal competitions, and Down Under is where you'll find cow racing, pig racing, cockroach racing, lizard racing, sheep racing, cane toad racing, and yabby racing, which involves a species of freshwater crustacean. Meanwhile, dog sled racing and chuckwagon racing can be considered modern versions of chariot races, with animals pulling a human on a vehicle.

Rodeos represent another interesting human–animal dichotomy in that humans both team with animals in some events (e.g., trick riding and barrel racing) and compete against them in others (e.g., calf roping and bronc busting). "This array of relationships falls on a continuum; one end is defined by human–animal cooperation, harmony, tameness, and control while the other end by conflict, violence, wildness, and unruliness," write sociologists Arnold Arluke and Robert Bogdan, adding that historically organizers who schedule rodeo events have taken this continuum into consideration, often building the program so it begins with the tame and ends with the wild.[2]

It should come as no surprise that a sport with deep roots in animal agriculture would have abuse built right into it. In assessing the various rodeo competitions, Peggy W. Larson, a former large-animal veterinarian and bareback bronc rider, says that roping events are the cruelest:

In calf roping, baby calves are used. If they were not in the rodeo, these calves would still be with their mothers on pasture. Weighing less than 300 pounds, they are forced to run at speeds in excess of 25 miles per hour when roped. The reason they run at such high speeds is that they are tormented in the holding chute: their tails are twisted, their tails are rubbed back and forth over the steel chute bars, and they are shocked with 5000-volt electric prods until the gate opens. They burst out of the chute at top speed only to be stopped short – or "clotheslined" – with a choking rope around the neck. They are often injured, and some are killed.[3]

Some of the other rodeo events that Dr. Larson identifies as particularly cruel include steer tripping, steer wrestling, bull riding, and bronc riding, all of which can result in the death of the animals used – and all in the name of "sport." She also points out how rodeos normalize violence toward animals, which can have a lasting impact on children. "Children who attend rodeos witness riders and ropers dominate and injure animals," she writes. "They see the spurs, the cattle prods and the ropes. They see brutal riders winning prizes. Animal abuse can become acceptable to them."[4]

The potential for desensitizing children to cruelty toward animals is also present in bullfighting. Indeed, in 2018, the United Nations Committee on the Rights of the Child urged Spain to ban anyone under 18 years of age from attending a bullfight or bullfighting school, describing the spectacle of bullfighting as "extreme violence."[5] Spanish officials ignored the suggestion, which is not terribly surprising since the country considers bullfighting to be a part of their cultural heritage – even a protected form of art.[6]

Hiding animal cruelty beneath the cloak of "art" is not a new tactic – visual artists who kill and then exhibit animals have been doing it for years – but trying to protect a barbarous practice like bullfighting by giving it special status is a callous approach to nationalism.

It would be easy enough to describe the cruelties of a bullfighting event, in which several bulls are generally slain – how the bulls are tormented, stabbed with spears, and ultimately killed with a sword before being dragged out of the bullring and butchered – but such details would probably come as no surprise to you. Instead, let's hear from someone who makes his living as an impartial travel guide and writer, visiting other countries and appreciating their customs. When Rick Steves attended a bullfight in Madrid, he was so appalled that he had to leave the arena soon after the killings began. He writes of encountering a couple from the Midwest, their daughter, and preteen son who also were also repulsed and left early. "The 12-year-old boy summed it up in three words: 'That was nasty.'" Steves' agreed with him. "It was nasty," he writes, adding that a bullfight "makes a spectacle out of the cruel killing of an animal."[7]

And let's hear from another bullfight observer: "I suppose, from a modern moral point of view, that is, a Christian point of view, the whole bullfight is indefensible; there is certainly much cruelty, there is always danger, either sought or unlooked for, and there is always death." Those are not the words of an animal rights activist but of Ernest Hemingway, perhaps the world's most celebrated bullfight aficionado. Even the man who arguably did more to elevate the practice of killing bulls for sport in the twentieth century than anyone else cannot look us in the eye and unconditionally defend this blood sport.[8]

The sentiment around bullfighting has gradually been changing. A few decades ago, anyone who spoke out against the blood sport in Spain risked suffering the wrath of bullfight supporters. But attendance has been declining every year, and today, polls show that Spanish society has become divided over the issue.[9] According one survey, more than two-thirds of Spanish people said they are "not very or not at all proud" of living in a country where bullfighting is a cultural tradition.[10]

Could it be that younger generations are recognizing that Nature is to be protected and not exploited?

One aspect of bullfighting that makes it rare among blood sports is that it pits a human against a nonhuman animal. More common are blood sports in which one or more nonhumans are set animal against another, such as dog fighting, cockfighting, bear baiting (dogs attacking a chained bear), and hare or rabbit coursing (dogs chasing and then killing a hare or rabbit). In these nature-vs-nature contests, the outcome is less certain – the hare may get away, the favored rooster may lose – but they demonstrate how some people perversely view animals as objects of amusement. In place of a relationship is objectification.

Not often considered a blood sport but certainly more in line with the human-conquering-nature philosophy are hunting and fishing. That humans have been preying upon animals since the Stone Age is considered indisputable. Killing animals was not sport for these early humans; it was survival. Later centuries found societies such as those in ancient Greece hunting for recreation and military practice; indeed, the Greek philosopher Aristotle believed that hunting animals was the first "just war" (that is, morally justifiable), while the Greek soldier Xenophon declared that it transformed young boys into ideal citizens and led to their success in battle.[11]

The hunt as a rite of passage that supposedly ensured masculinity has a long history, but it is not only boys and men who kill for sport these days. Many avid hunters consider the sport a family affair – a way for parents to bond with their children. They claim it is a great to teach kids respect for nature.

Yet killing someone is an odd way to teach respect, and such a life lesson does not always stick. As an example, take this response that some young hunters gave to an adult hunter when he asked what they planned to do with the squirrels they had shot: "We threw them away," one of the boys answered. "My dad says they're just rats, anyway."[12]

Not surprisingly, it has been found that children who are exposed to hunting become desensitized to animal cruelty, as those two boys had, and to violence in general.[13] Among the common experiences shared by teenage perpetrators of mass school shootings, for instance, is growing up in households in which a parent took them hunting as a child.[14]

Ironically, another of the motivations that hunters and fishers claim inspires them to kill animals is their desire to feel a kinship with wildlife. Whatever the justification, it is offered from an anthropocentric perspective, which regards humans as separate from and superior to nature. This viewpoint also happens to be central to many Western religions and philosophies, and from there it's easy to see how the use of animals in hunting and other sports would not only be popular but effortlessly excusable. (This is not to suggest that everyone who follows the tenets of Western religious practices ignores the divine that is present in the world around us.)

The eco-spiritualist, who recognizes the sacredness of nature and the intrinsic value in all life regardless of their usefulness to humans, rejects the anthropocentric attitude.

Perhaps it's no surprise that a lot of people who kill animals in the name of sport feel conflicted about what they do. "Everything wants to live, and will try anything it can to escape you," writes "outdoorsman" Hank Shaw. "We see ourselves in this struggle, feel tremendous empathy for the struggling bird, the fleeing deer. It is a soul-searing moment where part of you marvels at the animal's drive to live – to escape! – at the same time the rest of you is consumed with capturing it [sic] as fast as possible so you can end this miserable business. This internal conflict is, to me, what being human is all about."[15]

That hunters like Shaw can feel empathy for their prey gives me a little hope.

Endnotes

1. Judith Swaddling, *The Ancient Olympic Games*, second edition (University of Texas Press, 2008), pp. 83–87.

2. Arnold Arluke and Robert Bogdan, "Taming the Wild: Rodeo as a Human–Animal Metaphor," from *Sports, Animals, and Society*, edited by James Gillett and Michelle Gilbert (Routledge, 2014), pp. 15–19.

3. Peggy W. Larson, DVM, MS, JD, "Rodeos: Inherent Cruelty to Animals," Humane Society Veterinary Medical Association, January 15, 2015, https://www.hsvma.org/rodeos_inherent_cruelty_to_animals

4. Peggy W. Larson, DVM, MS, JD, "Rodeos: Inherent Cruelty to Animals," Humane Society Veterinary Medical Association,

January 15, 2015, https://www.hsvma.org/rodeos_inherent_cruelty_to_animals

5. Sam Jones, "Spain urged to ban children from bullfights," *The Guardian*, February 9, 2018, https://www.theguardian.com/world/2018/feb/08/un-panel-urges-spain-consider-banning-children-bullfights

6. Giles Tremlett, "Madrid protects bullfighting as an art form," *The Guardian*, March 6, 2010, https://www.theguardian.com/world/2010/mar/07/madrid-protects-bullfighting-art

7. Rick Steves, "A Trip to the Bullfight: Two Bulls Are Plenty," https://www.ricksteves.com/watch-read-listen/read/articles/two-bulls-are-plenty

8. Ernest Hemingway, *Death in the Afternoon* (Simon & Schuster, 2014), p. 1.

9. Raphael Minder, "Bullfighting, Already Ailing in Spain, Is Battered by Lockdown," *The New York Times*, June 21, 2020, https://www.nytimes.com/2020/06/21/world/europe/bullfighting-spain-coronavirus.html

10. Ewan Palmer, "'Bullfighting World is Important': Spain's Matadors Seek Bailout as Bulls Go Straight to Slaughterhouse Amid Pandemic," Newsweek.com, June 14, 2020, https://www.newsweek.com/spain-bullfighting-protest-coronavirus-1510743

11. Marti Kheel, *Nature Ethics: An Ecofeminist Perspective* (Rowman & Littlefield Publishers, Inc., 2008), p. 74.

12. Sonny Fulks, "Some Words On Respect For Nature And Hunting," *Press Pros Magazine*, October 11, 2020, https://pressprosmagazine.com/some-words-on-respect-for-nature-and-hunting/

13. Clifton P. Flynn, "Hunting and Illegal Violence Against Humans and Other Animals: Exploring the Relationship," *Society and Animals*, Volume 10, Number 2, July 2002, https://www.researchgate.net/publication/233599184_Hunting_and_Illegal_Violence_Against_Humans_and_Other_

Animals_Exploring_the_Relationship

14. Jorge Celis, "The Age of School Shootings: A Sociological Interpretation on Masculinity," *Actualidades Investigativas en Educación*, Volume 15, Number 1, 2015 https://www.scielo.sa.cr/scielo.php?script=sci_arttext&pid=S1409-47032015000100022

15. Hank Shaw, "On Killing," Honest-Food.net, December 7, 2011, https://honest-food.net/on-killing/

Chapter 5

Animals for Labor

This is what you shall do: Love the earth and sun and the animals.
– Walt Whitman

As interest in human–animal relationships grows, an example frequently offered as interspecies cooperation is that of people working alongside nonhuman animals. Yet "cooperation" implies that both parties are willingly engaged in and even benefitting equally from the work being performed, and this is rarely so with animals used for labor. One reason for this is that most of these animals are exploited for tasks that are considered too difficult, dangerous, or just inconvenient for humans to undertake; therefore, in many cases animals are forced to toil at the end of a whip or under the pain of even greater violence.

The level of violence often depends on whether or not the species is a domesticated and thus easily trained animal, such as a dog or horse, or an animal who, regardless of their apparent "tameness," retains a wild spirit, such as an elephant or monkey. Animals in this latter category may suffer exceptional cruelty. The training of elephants used to carry tourists in Thailand, for instance, begins when they are very young and have been snatched from their mothers. They are immobilized for days with chains and ropes between trees and posts or placed in a small container – known as a "crush" box – in which they cannot move. They are then beaten to break their spirit and make them compliant.[1]

Other forms of labor for which animals are used vary widely, from farming (oxen and water buffaloes), transport (camels, horses, donkeys, dogs), and sheep herding (dogs) to brick hauling (donkeys, mules, and horses), logging (elephants), and search and rescue (dogs). There is also a number of species used as service animals, who are trained to perform specific tasks and to work with people with disabilities, and therapy animals, who are trained to provide people with comfort and affection in stressful environments.

Although humans may profess to have formed a bond with some animals used for labor – as with the cop and their "K-9" partner – ultimately, they are not equals; the animal is a resource to be exploited. The military has a similar program using dogs as the police do (they call them military working dogs, or MWDs), and in both cases, the animals are put into danger (sniffing for bombs, for example, or going after an armed perpetrator) that no truly loving guardian would permit. Ultimately the animal is seen as a tool and given less consideration than their human counterpart.

The use of animals in the military is especially troubling. Even though they respond to the sounds of artillery and feel fear, they do not have a full awareness of the dangers they face. In addition to dogs, species pressed into combat throughout history include horses, elephants, pigeons, and cats. These animals have performed such battlefield tasks as carrying soldiers and munitions, relaying messages, evacuating the wounded, detecting booby traps, guarding camps, and locating improvised explosive devices.

Even with the advent of modern warfare, and its attendant planes and armored tanks, animals were forced to suffer the same miseries – or worse – as the troops in World War I, where an estimated 11 million horses, 200,000 pigeons, 100,000 dogs, and many other species were used. "There were more animals than men in many cavalry regiments," says Éric Baratay, a French historian whose work involves considering history from the perspective of animals. All the armies used animals, he says, though cultural differences meant they we treated differently. For example, British riders would take the time to unsaddle horses and even walk alongside them if they were tired, while the French often rode horses to the point of exhaustion. "On the British side was the idea that we are dealing with sentient beings and individual psychologies ... while on the French side, it was the model of [the animal as] machine that was paramount."[2]

About 8 million horses, mules, and donkeys lost their lives in the war, according to the charity Animal Aid. Although many of these animals were killed by shellfire, most of them perished from the inclement weather and appalling conditions. On the Western Front, the loss of British horses due to cold, hunger, exhaustion, and disease was about 200,000 – four times more than the 58,000 killed by enemy action.[3] "Almost nothing is known about pigeons and dogs," adds Baratay, because no reliable counts were kept on these animals.[4]

Animals continue to be exploited in conflicts, and as the world has changed, so have the ways we've used them. The US military has developed a very specialized class of dogs called Multi-Purpose Canines (MPCs), who are selected and trained to participate in stressful and dangerous operations, from sniffing out explosives and rappelling out of helicopters to parachuting from planes and chasing down human targets – all intended, in the words of the military, to "provide an extra layer of protection to the team."[5]

They mean the human team, of course. The dogs, while highly valued, are expendable. One such dog was Maiko. In 2018, the US Army used Maiko to secure a compound in Afghanistan, which caused Al Qaeda fighters to open fire, killing him.[6] Maiko was resoundingly praised as a hero.[7] One veteran's blog site went so far as to say that Maika "sacrificed himself," as though he understood the hazards he faced.[8]

Hundreds of dogs like Maiko are used by US and British Armed Forces, and while their fatalities are relatively low, we must ask ourselves if this "interspecies cooperation" is in their best interest, or does it merely serve a human purpose? Does it benefit the dog to put them through so much trauma that they could develop conditions similar to post-traumatic stress disorder (PTSD), a mental health condition that is triggered by a terrifying event? "While PTSD is not well understood in dogs, veterinarians, dog trainers, and specialists at Lackland Air Force Base agree that dogs show symptoms of combat stress as much as humans do," writes Sara Ohlms, a former dog handler with the Marine Corps. Although these animals may become fearful of loud noises and decide that they don't want to work, Ohlms says the military does everything it can to put them back into service – back into harm's way.[9]

A dog experiencing the horrors of combat is an obvious example of animals placed in danger, but species in many other environments are forced to perform work that is physically or emotionally hazardous. Among the most cheerless enterprises anywhere has to be the brick kiln industry, which hurts not only the donkeys, horses, and mules who strain beneath cumbersome burdens of bricks, but also people and the planet (brick kilns use coal and emit significant quantities of gaseous and particulate pollutants[10]). In South Asia, where bricks are commonly used for building construction, there are some 152,700 active brick kilns employing about 5 million people and using more than 500,000 animals[11] to produce 21 percent of the world's bricks.[12]

Here we get a glimpse of how the human–animal relationship can become mired in a cycle of dependence and misery. About two-thirds of brick kiln workers in South Asia are trapped in forced or bonded labor (having received a pay advance), enduring punishing heat, dusty and polluted air, tough terrains, and long hours.[13] Many of them live in extreme poverty and borrow money from the brick kiln owner for necessities such as healthcare or even to buy a donkey to work with them; if they are unable to repay their loans by the time they die, the debt is passed on to their child, who must pay it off by working at the kiln.[14]

Brick production involves a number of stages, from the molders who fashion clay into bricks to the kiln operators who fire and dry them. Every step of the way are the stackers, who move the bricks from point to point using animals. Many of the animals exploited in this industry live with their "owners" and are often used for work beyond the brick kilns of India, Pakistan, Nepal, and Afghanistan. One study found that 80 percent of the annual income earned by equine-owning families in the brick kilns was generated by their animals through the transport of bricks and 20 percent from other sources.[15] Animals are considered to be cheaper and more efficient than using small trucks or other mechanized vehicles, and they are able to negotiate the uneven terrain at the kiln sites.

The Donkey Sanctuary, a UK charity that aids equines in South Asia, has found donkeys with seeping wounds on their backs and legs, the result of being forced to carry heavy loads while their harnesses rubbed painfully on their raw wounds. One brick kiln worker who managed to purchase 27 donkeys had just six left – 21 had died in the kilns. He was literally working these animals to death.[16] The same organization reports that these animals have no access to clean water, are rarely given water during the day, are not allowed to graze, and are generally underfed for the work they do.[17]

There is a general feeling of discontent among humans in the brick kilns, and many understand that they share this unhappiness with their animals. "The donkeys are also suffering with us now for the work," said one worker participating in a study about donkey welfare in the brick kiln industry. "We really value them," said another, "because we eat our bread because of them."[18]

You'll find another economically disadvantaged population using animals for labor in Thailand, where monkeys are trained to pick coconuts. Although this practice is supposedly hundreds of years old, it's only become well-known in recent years as animal rights campaigners have brought attention to it. Videos readily available online show pig-tailed macaque monkeys fitted with metal collars and chained or tethered by rope; they nimbly scamper up coconut palm trees – some 100 feet tall – twist coconuts from branches, and let them drop to the ground.

The exploitation begins with poachers taking young monkeys from the wild and selling them to "monkey schools," where they learn the techniques necessary to pick up to 1,000 coconuts a day, six days a week – the monkeys work so much that one trainer admits they sometimes faint from exhaustion. And when they're not working, they are chained to tree stumps.[19] "The training of these monkeys always comes with pain," says Edwin Wiek, founder of the Wildlife Friends Foundation Thailand, a rescue center and sanctuary. "If you inflict pain, they'll quickly figure out what you want and obey your orders."[20]

There has been some debate over how widespread the practice of using monkeys to pick coconuts is in Thailand. The Thai government has said that most coconuts are picked by humans using a curved blade attached to a long pole and that the few farmers who do use monkeys only sell those products locally – they are not exported.[21]

But Arjen Schroevers, who runs a "humane" monkey school based on the Buddhist principles of compassion and nonviolence, disagrees. "It would be difficult to find a coconut product made in Thailand that wasn't picked by a monkey," he says, adding that monkeys pick 99 percent of the Thai coconuts sold for their oil and flesh.[22]

Wiek believes the practice has gone down sharply in recent years and estimates that there are now fewer than 3,000 macaques actively picking coconuts. "Looking at the scale of things," he says, "at all those tons and tons of coconuts being exported, it is a small part."[23]

What can we make of the human–animal relationship here?

Supposedly, many of the monkeys form close bonds with the farmers.[24] That's difficult to believe, assuming the animals are mistreated. It seems much more probable that the macaques are generally regarded as a means to an end. An article in the *Bangkok Post* reports that these animals "do not require social security and accident insurance. Monkeys are therefore considered a 'living machine' that is very valuable for coconut farmers."[25]

Perhaps we might find instructive the reaction of a particular monkey named Brother Kwan in the Thai Province of Nakhon Si Thammarat. Brother Kwan's "owner" reportedly would beat him when he showed any reluctance to climb a tree. One day, in retaliation, Brother Kwan threw a coconut at him from a high branch, striking the man on the head and killing him instantly.[26]

This chapter isn't meant to be a full examination of animals use for labor, any more than the other chapters offer a comprehensive look at their subjects; rather, it's intended to present a sampling of how people put animals to work for human benefit. One of those benefits is rarely covered in discussions like this one: physical assistance. That's probably because criticizing any effort to aid people with disabilities runs the risk of appearing at best insensitive and at worst ableist. But if one definition of *exploitation* is the act of using someone for your own advantage, then so-called "service animals" are indeed exploited.

Although dogs are the most common service animals, other species to be used include ferrets, capuchin monkeys, parrots, miniature horses, and potbellied pigs. But the biggest surprise in this category – both the species and how they assist humans – may be boa constrictors, who are trained to alert people with epilepsy by gently squeeze their neck if they sense a seizure coming on.[27]

Because dogs are the animals most often used, I will confine my commentary to them. Service dogs or assistance dogs, as they are known, perform a wide variety of tasks for the disabled, from helping children and adults with sensory and mobility impairments navigate the world to aiding those with mental illnesses by, say, bringing them medication or providing physical comfort during moments of distress.

Sadly, common techniques for training these dogs involve force, fear, and intimidation. "Too often we're not very nice to the dogs being trained," says Jennifer Arnold, founder of the US-based nonprofit Canine Assistants, which places service dogs with people with disabilities. "I'll just come out and say it – and expect to be attacked for saying it – but these dogs are slave labor. I don't know how else to put it. And it is the truth that no one talks about." Although positive reinforcement has been shown to be a more effective method, Arnold says some organizations continue to use cruel training techniques. "Perhaps, it's just because it's the way they've always done it, or maybe they believe it's faster," she says.[28]

Arnold is also critical of the method many organizations use to raise the dogs: after volunteers nurture them as puppies, housetrain them, and socialize them – in other words, develop a mutual attachment with them – the pups are suddenly moved back to the schools. "No one explains to the dogs what happened to the only family they've known," says Arnold. "These [puppy-raising] volunteers are wonderful, but is this [system] fair to the dogs?"[29] (I once knew such a volunteer, who would bring one dog after another into the office where we worked as part of each puppy's socialization. I asked him how he managed to bond with these animals and then just let them go after a few months, never to see them again. "It doesn't really bother me," he said, "but it is very upsetting for my wife.")

And while it once was true that service dog programs rescued the animals they trained from shelters, that is becoming increasingly rare as training now focuses more on purpose-bred dogs, who have demonstrated higher success rates than rescued dogs.[30]

However we view this controversial topic, it seems clear that service animals are placed in a situation that they did not choose. They are caregivers with very little freedom, and it's difficult to gauge how content and cared for they are, even if they are granted legal protections that other animals, even "pets," are not permitted, primarily because they share the protections of the humans they serve.[31]

So, how is someone supposed to mitigate the symptoms of their specific disability if not with a service animal, who may help them lead a more fulfilling life? Unfortunately, researchers have yet to create any good alternatives. Some fuss has been made over Microsoft's mobile, voice-based app Soundscape, which helps users who are blind or visually impaired move about unfamiliar environments, but it's not intended as a substitute for a guide dog, at least not in its current version. The lack of a non-animal solution does not negate the exploitation involved, however.

Responding to a question about service dogs on Quora.com, one person, who describes himself as "completely blind from birth," listed a number of reasons why he has no use for them, and the first was: "I've travelled on three continents using a cane and GPS software. I would gain no advantage by having a dog."[32] Plenty will disagree with his choice, of course, but it demonstrates that there are alternatives for some.

Whatever way we put animals to work for us, there is always an inherent inequity; it couldn't be otherwise when we are taking advantage of them. While we may be grateful for these animals, ultimately, they are tools we use to make our lives easier, and they suffer for it.

Endnotes

1. AFP, "Video shows abusive taming of Thai baby elephant," *Bangkok Post*, June 25, 2020, https://www.bangkokpost.com/

thailand/general/1940920/video-shows-abusive-taming-of-thai-baby-elephant

2. Stéphanie Trouillard, "The Great War's unsung four-legged heroes," France24, April 20, 2014, https://www.france24.com/en/20140420-great-wars-unsung-four-legged-heroes-animals-history-france-world-war

3. "War Horses," Animal Aid, https://www.animalaid.org.uk/wp-content/uploads/2016/11/Animals-in-WWI-War-Horses-factsheet.pdf

4. Email from Éric Baratay, August 14, 2021.

5. Cpl. Steven Fox, US Marine Corps Forces Special Operations Command, "MARSOC Multi-Purpose Canine Handlers Train for Unforeseen," Military.com, December 16, 2014, https://www.military.com/special-operations/2014/12/16/marsoc-multi-purpose-canine-handlers-train-for-unforeseen.html

6. Kyle Rempfer, "An Army Ranger dog was killed while saving soldiers' lives in Afghanistan," ArmyTimes.com, December 5, 2018, https://www.armytimes.com/news/your-army/2018/12/05/an-army-ranger-dog-was-killed-while-saving-soldiers-lives-in-afghanistan/

7. "Beloved Army Ranger Dog Died Protecting Soldiers," InsideEdition.com, December 5, 2018, https://www.insideedition.com/beloved-army-ranger-dog-died-protecting-soldiers-48957

8. Matthew Russell, "Military Working Dog Sacrificed Himself To Save Army Rangers In Afghanistan," https://blog.theveteranssite.greatergood.com/maiko-ranger/

9. Sara Ohlms, "This is why Navy SEALs and Delta Force take dogs on capture-kill missions against terrorist leaders," Insider.com, October 31, 2019, https://www.insider.com/how-us-military-trains-dogs-navy-seal-delta-force-missions-2019-10

10. Bhat Mohd Skinder, Ashok K. Pandit, et al., "Brick kilns: Cause of Atmospheric Pollution," *Journal of Pollution Effects*

& *Control*, Volume 2, Issue 2, 2014, https://www.longdom.
org/open-access/brick-kilns-cause-of-atmospheric-
pollution-2375-4397.1000112.pdf

11. Dakhina Mitra and Delphine Valette, "Brick by Brick:
Unveiling the Full Picture of South Asia's Brick Kiln
industry and Building the Blocks for Change," International
Labour Organization, The Brooke Hospital for Animals, and
The Donkey Sanctuary, 2017, https://www.thebrooke.org/
sites/default/files/Brooke%20News/Brick-by-Brick-Report.
pdf An estimated 380,000 animals are working in the kilns
in India and more than 115,000 in Pakistani brick kilns.
About 6,900 working equine animals are found in the brick
kilns provinces of Kabul, Herat, Mazar, and Nangharar in
Afghanistan, while there are more than 2,200 of them in
Nepal, the majority of whom are working in the Kathmandu
Valley.

12. Andrew Eil, Jie Li, Prajwal Baral, and Eri Saikawa, "Dirty
Stacks, High Stakes: An Overview of Brick Sector in South
Asia," World Bank, 2020, https://documents1.worldbank.
org/curated/en/685751588227715919/pdf/Dirty-Stacks-
High-Stakes-An-Overview-of-Brick-Sector-in-South-Asia.
pdf

13. DaMitra and Valette, "Brick by Brick: Unveiling the Full
Picture of South Asia's Brick Kiln industry and Building the
Blocks for Change."

14. Faras Ghani, "The spiralling debt trapping Pakistan's brick
kiln workers," Al Jazeera, October 21, 2019, https://www.
aljazeera.com/features/2019/10/21/the-spiralling-debt-
trapping-pakistans-brick-kiln-workers

15. DaMitra and Valette, "Brick by Brick: Unveiling the Full
Picture of South Asia's Brick Kiln industry and Building the
Blocks for Change."

16. "Brick kilns of neglect in Nepal," June 11, 2018, https://
www.thedonkeysanctuary.org.uk/news/life-and-death-in-

nepals-brick-kilns/brick-kilns-of-neglect-in-nepal

17. DaMitra and Valette, "Brick by Brick: Unveiling the Full Picture of South Asia's Brick Kiln industry and Building the Blocks for Change."

18. Tamlin L. Watson, Laura M. Kubasiewicz, et al., "Cultural 'Blind Spots,' Social Influence and the Welfare of Working Donkeys in Brick Kilns in Northern India," *Frontiers in Veterinary Science*, Volume 7, Number 214, April 29, 2020, https://www.ncbi.nlm.nih.gov/pmc/articles/PMC7201042/

19. Nanchanok Wongsamuth, "Pay coconuts, get monkeys," *Bangkok Post*, September 6, 2015, https://www.bangkokpost. com/thailand/special-reports/681936/pay-coconuts-get-monkeys

20. Patrick Winn, "Does Thailand have a monkey labor problem?" The World, August 26, 2020, https://www.pri. org/stories/2020-08-26/does-thailand-have-monkey-labor-problem

21. Tassanee Vejpongsa, "Thailand denies monkeys abused to harvest coconut products," *Washington Post*, July 7, 2020, https://www.washingtonpost.com/world/europe/thailand -denies-monkeys-abused-to-harvest-coconut-products/2020/ 07/07/142f4dc4-c026-11ea-8908-68a2b9eae9e0_story.html

22. Eliza Barclay, "What's Funny About The Business Of Monkeys Picking Coconuts?" NPR, October 19, 2015, https:// www.npr.org/sections/thesalt/2015/10/19/448960760/ monkeys-pick-coconuts-in-thailand-are-they-abused-or-working-animals

23. Winn, "Does Thailand have a monkey labor problem?"

24. Adolfo Arranz, "Coconut harvesters or slaves?" South China Morning Post, July 29, 2020, https://multimedia.scmp.com/ infographics/news/world/article/3094954/coconut-harvest/

25. Nanchanok Wongsamuth, "Pay coconuts, get monkeys."

26. Andrew Drummond, "Monkey gets revenge on owner who forced him to climb trees for coconuts... by killing him with a

well-aimed coconut," *The Daily Mail*, March 10, 2009, https://
www.dailymail.co.uk/news/article-1160901/Monkey-gets-
revenge-owner-forced-climb-trees-coconuts--killing-aimed-
coconut.html

27. Linda Marx, "Pet Snake's Job Is to Sense His Owner's
Seizures," People.com, January 21, 2010, https://people.
com/pets/pet-snakes-job-is-to-sense-his-owners-seizures/

28. Steve Dale, "Assistance Dogs May Be Well Cared For, But
Are They Happy," March 7, 2014, https://stevedalepetworld.
com/blog/assistance-dogs-may-be-well-cared-for-but-are-
they-happy/

29. Dale, "Assistance Dogs May Be Well Cared For, But Are
They Happy."

30. Margo DeMello, *Animals and Society: An Introduction to
Human–Animal Studies* (Columbia University Press, 2012), p.
209.

31. John J. Ensminger, *Service and Therapy Dogs in American
Society: Science, Law and the Evolution of Canine Caregivers*
(Charles C. Thomas, 2010), p. 43.

32. Chris Meredith, "Why don't some blind people have
service animals?" https://www.quora.com/Is-using-guide-
dogs-to-help-blind-people-cruel-Are-there-alternatives-
It%E2%80%99s-fine-for-the-human-but-are-the-dogs-ever-
rewarded-for-their-work-Who-gives-them-exercise-lets-
them-off-their-leash-feeds-them-shows-them-love-plays-
catch-with-them

Chapter 6

Animals We Revere

That which extends throughout the universe I regard as my body and that which directs the universe I consider my own nature. All people are my brothers and sisters, and all things are my companions.
– Zhang Zai

As I sit at my desk and consider that special class of animals – those humans revere – two small rabbits are asleep just a few feet away. My wife, Lauren, and I rescued them not long ago: we found them abandoned in a nearby neighborhood. We managed to catch them and bring them home, where we are giving them the care they deserve and gradually gaining their trust. They remind me now that even some people who proclaim to "love" animals can struggle with that concept.

And yet, domesticated animals have an enormous capacity for forgiveness. These two little rabbits, probably not yet six months old, have clearly experienced some of the worst in human nature, and I hope that as we continue to foster them, they will understand that people can indeed be a source of love and protection. Soon they will be adopted into a permanent home, which will be a bittersweet adjustment for us but the beginning of what we hope will be long and wonderful lives for them.

That has become humanity's covenant with dogs, cats, rabbits, and other animals most people refer to as "pets." We domesticate them from their wild cousins, breed them, and share our households with them. They give us unconditional love, and in exchange we make sure their needs are met. These are the fortunate one percent of animals who, within a given society, humans generally do not kill for food or clothing. Instead, we open our homes and hearts to them, creating a bond that is probably what first comes to mind for most us when we think of the human–animal relationship. Pampered and loved, companion animals are treated with dignity and respect. They are family.

As wonderful as companion animals are, they present a set of problems, beginning with breeding. The entire domestication process of animals we now call pets took hundreds or even thousands of years of goal-oriented breeding to ensure a line of animals with characteristics that are compatible with humans. Breeders continue the practice today by mating a male and female – the animals rarely have a choice in whom they mate with. At best, the exploitation and manipulation of their behaviors and reproductive systems is unfair to the dogs, cats, and rabbits, and at worst, the animals are part of a highly abusive and irresponsible industry: "puppy mills," "kitten mills," "rabbit mills," and other large-scale, commercial breeding facilities that churn out pets for profit.

Not only are many of these animals born with health issues, but the entire breeding industry contributes to the overpopulation of pets, millions of whom are housed in shelters and euthanized every year. Even a pet born without any apparent health problems can eventually suffer because of selective breeding. Lop-eared rabbits, for instance, are enormously popular with children, yet breeding for this purely aesthetic trait leaves them prone to painful ear and dental discomfort.[1]

Moreover, the practice of keeping pets is problematic because it denies animals the right of self-determination. They have no choice in where they live, whom they live with, what they eat, or if they retain their reproductive organs. Even where (and sometimes when) they relieve themselves is dictated by others.

As the popularity of keeping companion animals grows, so too does humanity's attachment to them. There are more pets than people in the US – nearly 400 million at last count, giving every two out of three households a companion animal. And

95 percent of people in the country consider their pets to be family.[2] Other countries where companion animals are treated as members of the family include Canada (95 percent),[3] Great Britain (90 percent),[4] Italy (80 percent),[5] New Zealand (76 percent),[6] and Australia (60 percent).[7]

Meanwhile, it seems that every day we are learning that the inner lives of these animals are a lot more complex than we once thought. Dogs, for instance, experience not only love, anger, fear, grief, anxiety, and joy, but also more nuanced emotions such as shame, embarrassment, jealousy, guilt, resentment, pride, and empathy – and they can identify these feelings in humans by observing us.[8] "The logical consequence is that the more we attribute them with these characteristics, the less right we have to control every single aspect of their lives," says researcher Hal Herzog, who specializes in human–animal relations.[9]

Most people clearly revere their companion animals, and this may be one of the least exploitive relationships humans can have with another species – there are, after all, elements of mutual affection here. If society is to continue the institution of pet keeping, then we owe it to these animals to reduce our reliance on pet breeders by adopting from shelters and rescue groups.

Keeping Wild Animals as Pets

Not everyone is content with having a dog, cat, rabbit, or other domesticated animals as a pet. For some, it is much more interesting to "own" a wild animal. In most cases, this is illegal – not to mention inhumane – but that doesn't stop those whose idea of getting closer to nature involves participating in wildlife trafficking and keeping an animal at home as a living trophy. The practice is so widespread that there are now more tigers living in captivity in the United States than there are in the wild: according to the World Wildlife Fund, while there are some 3,900 free-living tigers around the world, an estimated 5,000 of the big cats live in captivity in the US.[10]

Having a wild animal as a pet routinely ends up harming humans, and animals pay the price. A 200-pound chimpanzee named Buck, for example, lived for 17 years at an Oregon home when he suddenly attacked his owner's daughter in 2021, biting her arms, legs, and torso. When the police arrived, they shot Buck to death.[11] In 2009, a 350-pound black bear named Teddy killed his owner as she was cleaning his cage in Pennsylvania; a neighbor then gunned down Teddy.[12] Game wardens killed a 500-pound deer in Texas after he trampled and gored his owner to death in 2011.[13]

That we want to keep wild animals in our homes is an indication of how much we admire them. Indeed, even if we don't share our homes with any animals, a growing number of people are getting out in nature to watch wildlife – and they are beginning to outnumber those for whom experiencing the great outdoors means killing animals. In 1960, a survey found almost 14 million licensed hunters in the United States, making it among the most popular outdoor activities in the country.[14] But six decades later, it has not kept pace with changing demographics. The US has nearly twice the population, but about the same number of people hunting. In contrast, more than 20 million people participate in wildlife viewing.[15]

Such an interest in wildlife has helped make ecotourism one of the fastest-growing sectors of the travel industry. This is recreation directed toward natural areas that conserve the environment and that sustains the well-being of the local people. Observing flora and fauna while respecting the principles of conservation sounds great, right? And it is. But there are also downsides, which may impact the very animals ecotourism is supposed to safeguard. One study found that no matter how good their intentions and practices, a traveler's presence can harm wildlife by habituating them to humans.[16] Prey animals, for example, may become less vigilant, making them easier targets for both predators and poachers. "Ecotourists, in theory, are trying to do good things to protect biodiversity; they're trying not to trample plants or startle wildlife," says Daniel Blumstein co-author of the study and chair of ecology and evolutionary biology at the University of California–Los Angeles. "But many are completely unaware of their impact. People can't go to these areas and not have an impact."[17]

Venturing into the wilderness to connect with nature also leads to increased foot traffic, which can damage an area's ecosystem by impacting soil quality and plant life and even trampling small animals. Moreover, consequences that sometimes accompany ecotourism – including visitor trash, the introduction of diseases, and the presence of land and water vehicles – all add to the ecological burden.[18]

Ocean Life

The ocean is an environment of extremes, hosting arguably the world's smallest animal – the microscopic zooplankton – and the largest – the blue whale, reaching up to 100 feet long and 200 tons. Animals living here hold a unique place in humanity's pantheon of revered species, as these individuals are outwardly so unlike us and yet so admired. With faces that offer almost no discernible expressions and body language that is nearly impossible to decipher, they nonetheless captivate us with their beauty and gracefulness. Many of these aquatic animals – in particular whales, dolphins, porpoises, sharks, seals, turtles, and sea lions – have been the subject of much of our popular culture. They have played heroes (and sometimes villains) in literature, movies, and television; they have been featured in songs and poetry; and they have even been worshipped as divine beings living on Earth.

Although marine animals are vastly different from humans, some are admittedly like us in significant ways, especially cetaceans – whales, dolphins, and porpoises. These animals are highly social with complex relationships, and they communicate with regional dialects. They play, use tools, and share the responsibility of raising their young within their social group. Dolphins may even gossip.[19] Perhaps most importantly, they also possess self-awareness, a quality that only a few species have been found to share with humans.[20] Although the scientific definition of self-awareness is the ability of an animal to recognize themselves in a mirror, it is becoming more widely accepted that animals are sentient beings – that is, that they are conscious and experience a full range of emotions, from joy and pleasure to pain and fear. Such is certainly the case with fishes, crustaceans, mollusks, and marine mammals.[21, 22]

As we embrace the emerging conviction that aquatic animals do in fact think, feel, and know that they exist, let's contemplate for a moment the practice of keeping cetaceans in captivity. The tradition began in 1861 with the capture of a beluga whale, who was exhibited at the Boston Aquarial Gardens and survived for a year and a half amid salt water pumped in from Boston Harbor. In New York City, P.T. Barnum popularized cetaceans as a spectacle by displaying two beluga whales in 1861, and they reportedly enthralled patrons of his museum – until they died two days later. Barnum replaced them with others, and they also quickly perished. So expendable did Barnum consider these animals that he used their impending deaths as a way to entice customers, boasting in one 1865 advertisement: "NOW IS THE TIME to see these wonders as THEIR LIVES ARE UNCERTAIN, seven of the same species having died while being exhibited at this Museum."[23]

These early ventures in displaying a species people had previously thought impossible to maintain in captivity were set against the backdrop of the 19th century, when an expanding network of railroads and ocean-going ships made the world seem smaller and nature less frightening. In the US, the wilderness was rapidly giving way to development, industrial employers were reducing work hours, and the lower and middle classes now had a little time for leisure activities. Similar trends were occurring in Great Britain and elsewhere in Europe. People were able to enjoy a day off, and many of them wanted to see exotic animals like whales.

Whether or not we can say that humans have been successful in keeping cetaceans in captivity is a matter of opinion. Yes, many orcas, dolphins, beluga whales, and others have been caught and put on display in marine parks and aquaria. And, yes, they now live a bit longer than in Barnum's day. But they still lead, to put it bluntly, terrible, unnaturally short lives in tragically small tanks. This hasn't stopped abusement park owners, of course, who understand that the public is fascinated by these species and that their desire to show how much they "love" animals – by paying to see them confined in an artificial environment – is a gold mine.

One alternative to captivity that has become increasingly popular is whale watching. Observing whales and dolphins in their natural environment is indeed thrilling. Yet, like other forms of nature tourism, this option has its own set of problems, since the presence of boats and their loud motors can disrupt the animals' ability to communicate, raise their young, and forage for food. This has led to so-called "ethical" watching in which tour operators minimize their impact on whales and dolphins – even using silent boats that run on electricity. Another alternative is a virtual reality experience in which the animals are digital creations projected onto high-definition screens. I saw one of the first such interactive attractions on Phillip Island, Australia, recently, and the result is incredibly lifelike.

Sanctuaries

In an ideal world, there would be no animal sanctuaries. Humans would live in perfect harmony with other species, and we would have no need to rescue animals from cases of abuse, neglect, and abandonment. Until human–animal relationships have evolved to that point, however, we can be thankful that organizations exist to provide a permanent home and quality care for the neglected and exploited. In these havens, animals are given the freedom to be themselves, and while there may be some limit to the space they are provided – no sanctuary could give, say, an elephant or lion the same independence they would enjoy in the African savanna – they are nevertheless able to live out the remainder of their lives in safety.

Not all sanctuaries are bastions of ethical practices, but the best facilities take into account the animals' social needs as well as their physical requirements. And they come in many forms, including those that rescue farmed animals and educate consumers about problems with animal agriculture, those that provide animals liberated from circuses and zoos a life free from chains and fear, and those that focus on a specific species, such as elephants, cats, or koalas. Much has been written elsewhere about why some sanctuaries are "good" and others are "bad"; rather than wade into that debate, I'll explore for a moment why they are important.

Sanctuaries are extensions of our reverence for animals. They remind us that we can and should care for the beings with whom we share this planet, and they give us at least a glimpse of how animals behave in an environment that is absent the attendant stressors of captivity, factory farming, tourism, or wherever else they were rescued from. Sanctuaries can serve many important functions. Some protect endangered species, for instance, while at farmed animal sanctuaries, cows, pigs, chickens, turkeys, ducks, rabbits, goats, sheep, and other liberated animals are ambassadors of their species, reminding people not only of the horrors of the food system but that animals deserve rights.

While some sanctuaries are built from the ground up, others are created beneath the waves. These marine sanctuaries not only offer secure habitats to ocean-dwelling species nearing extinction, such as sea turtles and blue whales, but to kelp forests, seagrass beds, and even shipwrecks. In fact, the first national marine sanctuary in the US was designated in 1975 to protect the wreck of the Civil War ironclad *USS Monitor*, which is a rather sad commentary on human priorities. The largest marine sanctuary, so far, is a 600,000-square-mile reserve (twice the size of Texas) off the coast of Antarctica in the Ross Sea. In effect as of 2017, the sanctuary is the first to be designated in international waters and came after years of negotiation among 24 countries. It demonstrates the willingness of governments to put the interests of orcas and penguins ahead of their own, though only temporarily: unless the agreement is renewed, the protections will expire in 2052.

We create these sanctuaries because we care what happens to animals and the planet. They are a safe space as well as a critical educational tool, helping people understand how human habits and activities affect the lives of non-human animals. Visiting a sanctuary for farmed animals, for example, can be a powerful motivation for embracing veganism.

Animals are better versions of us; by observing them, we learn a healthier way of living – even a kinder way of being. We are only beginning to understand them, and yet it seems clear that animals have a moral edge over humanity. They do not imprison other animals, for instance. They do not litter nature with garbage. They do not contribute to climate change or habitat destruction or species extinction. If an animal does not like you, they will tell you so – there is no deceit; likewise, their love is unconditional.

Apologists of animal exploitation excel at excusing their practices by arguing that humans are not only different but superior and therefore deserving of better treatment. It does appear that we are superior at defending any behavior that is to our benefit. Yet perhaps it is the Homo sapiens' inability to reconcile our contradictory nature – the way we're able to see some animals as useful tools and others as beloved family members – that truly sets us apart from other species.

As I was researching and writing this chapter, one of the two rabbits I mentioned in the first paragraph died. She suffered a host of complications after her spay surgery and was in a lot of pain. There was no way her life could be saved, so Lauren and I agreed with her veterinarian that the most compassionate decision was to euthanize her. We were heartbroken, especially for her mate, who was so devoted to and protective of her. We brought him to the clinic so he could say goodbye with us. It may seem surprising how attached we can become to animals after so short a time, but such is the bond we share. We've since adopted the male and named him Bunito.

Endnotes

1. "Lop-eared rabbits more likely to have tooth/ear problems than erect eared cousins," *Science Daily*, October 1, 2019, https://www.sciencedaily.com/releases/2019/10/191001184929.htm
2. Celia Miller, "Pet Ownership Statistics," Spots.com, July 28, 2021, https://spots.com/pet-ownership-statistics/
3. https://pawzy.co/blog/fun/pets-part-of-the-family-Canadian-survey
4. "Pets Considered Part Of The Family, Census Shows," Sky News, August 25, 2013, https://news.sky.com/story/pets-considered-part-of-the-family-census-shows-10436356
5. https://www.statista.com/statistics/1055937/pet-owners-considering-their-pet-as-a-family-member-in-italy/
6. https://static1.squarespace.com/static/5d1bf13a3f8e880001289eeb/t/5f768e8a17377653bd1eebef/1601605338749/Companion+Animals+in+NZ+2020+%281%29.pdf
7. https://kb.rspca.org.au/knowledge-base/how-many-pets-are-there-in-australia/
8. Marc Bekoff, Ph D, *Canine Confidential: Why Dogs Do What They Do* (The University of Chicago Press, 2018), p. 136.

9. Linda Rodriguez McRobbie, "Should we stop keeping pets? Why more and more ethicists say yes," *The Guardian*, August 1, 2017, https://www.theguardian.com/lifeandstyle/2017/aug/01/should-we-stop-keeping-pets-why-more-and-more-ethicists-say-yes

10. Faith Karimi, "There are more tigers in captivity in the US than in the wild," CNN, May 13, 2021, https://www.cnn.com/2021/05/13/us/tigers-captive-us-wild-trnd/index.html

11. Josh K. Elliott, "Pet chimpanzee shot dead after attacking owner's daughter," Global News, June 22, 2021, https://globalnews.ca/news/7970302/chimpanzee-attack-woman-shot-oregon/

12. Michael Rubinkam, "Pet bear turns on Pa. owner, kills her in cage," Associated Press, October 5, 2009, https://www.seattletimes.com/nation-world/pet-bear-turns-on-pa-owner-kills-her-in-cage/

13. David Ingram, "500 pound deer kept in backyard kennel kills owner" KBMT, November 27, 2011, https://www.12newsnow.com/article/news/500-pound-deer-kept-in-backyard-kennel-kills-owner/270341929

14. Edward Putnam, "Is Wildlife Viewing the New Hunting?" *Backcountry Journal*, Winter 2017, https://www.backcountryhunters.org/is_wildlife_viewing_the_new_hunting_backcountry_journal_excerpt

15. https://www.statista.com/statistics/191348/participants-in-wildlife-viewing-in-the-us-since-2006/

16. Daniel T. Blumstein, Benjamin Geffroy, et al., "How Nature-Based Tourism Might Increase Prey Vulnerability to Predators," *Trends in Ecology & Evolution*, Volume 30, Issue 12, December 1, 2015, https://www.cell.com/trends/ecology-evolution/fulltext/S0169-5347(15)00246-3?_returnURL=

17. Gregory Barber, "No, Your Eco-Vacation Is Not Actually Doing Animals Any Favors," *Mother Jones*, October 12, 2015, https://www.motherjones.com/environment/2015/10/are-

we-making-wildlife-dumber/

18. Graeme Shannon, Courtney L. Larson, et al., "Ecological Consequences of Ecotourism for Wildlife Populations and Communities," from *Ecotourism's Promise and Peril: A Biological Evaluation*, edited by Daniel T. Blumstein, Benjamin Geffroy, et al. (Springer International Publishing, 2017), pp. 29–46.

19. Katharina Kropshofer, "Whales and dolphins lead 'human-like lives' thanks to big brains, says study," *The Guardian*, October 16, 2017, https://www.theguardian.com/science/2017/oct/16/whales-and-dolphins-human-like-societies-thanks-to-their-big-brains

20. As of the publication of this book, those species include bottlenose dolphins, orcas, bonobos, orangutans, chimpanzees, Asian elephants, magpies, pigeons, ants, and the cleaner wrasse fish.

21. Instituto Gulbenkian de Ciencia, "Emotional states discovered in fish," Phys.org, October 30, 2017, https://phys.org/news/2017-10-emotional-states-fish.html

22. Lynne U Sneddon, "Pain in aquatic animals," *The Journal of Experimental Biology*, Volume 218, Number 7, 2015, https://pubmed.ncbi.nlm.nih.gov/25833131/

23. https://lostmuseum.cuny.edu/archive/ad-for-whales-july-2-1865

About the Author

Mark Hawthorne is a longtime animal advocate and ethical vegan. His other books include *The Way of the Rabbit*, *A Vegan Ethic: Embracing A Life Of Compassion Toward All*, *Bleating Hearts: The Hidden World of Animal Suffering*, and the bestselling *Striking at the Roots: A Practical Guide to Animal Activism*, which was updated as a tenth-anniversary edition in 2018. Mark is a frequent contributor to *VegNews* magazine, and he volunteers with the vegan food justice group Food Empowerment Project. He and his partner, Lauren, live in Northern California with an adorable rabbit named Bunito. You can read more of Mark's writing at MarkHawthorne.com

Other books in the *Earth Spirit* series

Belonging to the Earth
Nature Spirituality in a Changing World
Julie Brett
978-1-78904-969-5 (Paperback)
978-1-78904-970-1 (ebook)

Confronting the Crisis
Essays and Meditations on Eco-Spirituality
David Sparenberg
978-1-78904-973-2 (Paperback)
978-1-78904-974-9 (ebook)

Environmental Gardening
Think Global Act Local
Elen Sentier
978-1-78904-963-3 (Paperback)
978-1-78904-964-0 (ebook)

Healthy Planet
Global Meltdown or Global Healing
Fred Hageneder
978-1-78904-830-8 (Paperback)
978-1-78904-831-5 (ebook)

Honoring the Wild
Reclaiming Witchcraft and Environmental Activism
Irisanya Moon
978-1-78904-961-9 (Paperback)
978-1-78904-962-6 (ebook)

Saving Mother Ocean
We all need to help save the seas!
Steve Andrews
978-1-78904-965-7 (Paperback)
978-1-78904-966-4 (ebook)

The Circle of Life is Broken
An Eco-Spiritual Philosophy of the Climate Crisis
Brendan Myers
978-1-78904-977-0 (Paperback)
978-1-78904-978-7 (ebook)

MOON
BOOKS

PAGANISM & SHAMANISM

What is Paganism? A religion, a spirituality, an alternative belief system, nature worship? You can find support for all these definitions (and many more) in dictionaries, encyclopaedias, and text books of religion, but subscribe to any one and the truth will evade you. Above all Paganism is a creative pursuit, an encounter with reality, an exploration of meaning and an expression of the soul. Druids, Heathens, Wiccans and others, all contribute their insights and literary riches to the Pagan tradition. Moon Books invites you to begin or to deepen your own encounter, right here, right now.

If you have enjoyed this book, why not tell other readers by posting a review on your preferred book site.

Journey to the Dark Goddess
How to Return to Your Soul
Jane Meredith
Discover the powerful secrets of the Dark Goddess and
transform your depression, grief and pain into healing
and integration.
Paperback: 978-1-84694-677-6 ebook: 978-1-78099-223-5

Shamanic Reiki
Expanded Ways of Working with Universal Life Force Energy
Llyn Roberts, Robert Levy
Shamanism and Reiki are each powerful ways of healing; together,
their power multiplies. *Shamanic Reiki* introduces techniques to
help healers and Reiki practitioners tap ancient healing wisdom.
Paperback: 978-1-84694-037-8 ebook: 978-1-84694-650-9

Pagan Portals – The Awen Alone
Walking the Path of the Solitary Druid
Joanna van der Hoeven
An introductory guide for the solitary Druid, *The Awen Alone* will
accompany you as you explore, and seek out your own place
within the natural world.
Paperback: 978-1-78279-547-6 ebook: 978-1-78279-546-9

A Kitchen Witch's World of Magical Herbs & Plants
Rachel Patterson
A journey into the magical world of herbs and plants, filled with
magical uses, folklore, history and practical magic. By popular
writer, blogger and kitchen witch, Tansy Firedragon.
Paperback: 978-1-78279-621-3 ebook: 978-1-78279-620-6